The Myths of Toxic Femininity

Causes, Consequences and Cure

Van Thanh Binh

Stephen Whitehead

Acorn Books
www.acornbooks.uk

Published in 2025 by
Acorn Books
An Imprint of
Andrews UK Limited
West Wing Studios
Unit 166, The Mall
Luton, LU1 2TL

Copyright © 2025
Van Thanh Binh
with Stephen Whitehead

Contents

About the Authors

Van Thanh Binh is a Vietnamese academic and researcher into self-love. She is Lecturer in Emotional Intelligence, Self-Love and Literature of English-Speaking Countries at the University of Languages and International Studies, Vietnam National University, Hanoi.

Dr Stephen Whitehead is a British sociologist, best-selling author and internationally recognized expert on men and masculinities, gender and identity, education and inclusivity. This is Stephen's eighteenth book. Stephen's website is www.stephen-whitehead.com

For our families

Part One: Causes

Chapter One: Context

Our original version of this book was published in February 2024 under the title: *Self-Love for Women: overcoming toxic femininity and suffering.*

This new version, published a year later, delves more deeply into toxic femininity and the myths informing it, while holding true to the concept of Totally Inclusive Self-Love as the cure for this ubiquitous gender virus. In addition, this version introduces the concept of independent femininity and links it to self-love. The twelve stories of women around the world who have suffered from – and in some cases overcome – toxic femininity, remain for the most part identical to the original book.

So why produce a revised book with more emphasis on toxic femininity?

Because global attention is now turning towards toxic femininity. While this is inevitable, concern arises when commentators – especially men – uncritically and unreflectively, in some cases maliciously, use the term toxic femininity to attack women, the intention being to deflect attention from the problematic behaviour of men, especially that which is now globally recognised as toxic masculinity.

As we detail in the following pages, toxic femininity and toxic masculinity are not the same thing though they certainly originate from the same place – patriarchal values and male-ist cultures intended to privilege men and assert men's power over women.

The narratives of the twelve women detailed in this book provide the unequivocal evidential base for our concept of toxic femininity. Therefore, in our estimation, any alternative definition of toxic femininity that seeks to posit it as the female equivalent of toxic masculinity is not only simplistic but comprehensively wrong, not least because such a superficial definition fails to politically contextualise gender relationships.

If these twelve accounts of real lives were in themselves to be considered inconclusive evidence as to the hegemonic potential of toxic femininity, then one might simply invite any woman anywhere to reflect on this question:

> *In what ways have you been pressured through your life to conform to traditional/patriarchal gender practices, expectations and values even while such would result in limiting your actions, opportunities and life choices?*

The answers that women give to this question would show that we could have filled many books with the stories of women struggling with toxic femininity. For is not every woman's life in part a battle against male-ist cultures and gender stereotypes and therefore a quest for independence? And by independence we mean independence from men and from the pressure to be subject to male power and its dictates, not least through male intimidation, threats, coercion and violence.

That said, there are crucial differences between women that must be acknowledged, not least differences in the intersectional constitution of their identity and how they experience and express that identity in public and private settings. Toxic femininity can impact women in various and multiple ways depending, for example, on their upbringing, sexuality, education, race, age, ethnicity and social class. No two women are exactly alike; they do not experience toxic femininity in exactly the same way nor grapple with exactly the same array of problems which can arise from this discursive virus. Nor do all women succumb to toxic femininity, at least without a fight. But what remains common to all females is that the myths and discourses informing toxic femininity will be placed before them in the expectation they get taken up as identity constructs. In many parts of the world that pressure is explicit and reinforced through education, law, culture, intimidation and violence.

The twelve stories detailed in this book reveal these differences together with the ubiquitous and insidious social pressure overlaying traditional gender narratives. The stories are representative and illustrative of three types of woman:

1. Those who are overwhelmed by this condition

2. Those who spend much of their life battling against it

3. Those who triumph over it.

Using these twelve stories as extended case studies, this book has three aims:

1. To name toxic femininity, identify the myths which inform it and call out its malign influence over women around the world

2. To name an emergent femininity in global society – independent femininity

3. To show how to use Totally Inclusive Self-Love to overcome all suffering, including that generated by toxic femininity and gendered cultures.

3

The Women in This Book

Each woman portrayed in this book is a living and breathing soul. She exists in the world at time of writing. Her story is not contrived but it has been anonymised. We have applied some artistic licence in some places in some stories and in some instances blended elements from other women's stories not revealed in the book – though not enough to alter or corrode the essence of the story nor shift the narrative.

These are twelve individual women and as you will see they are fascinatingly unique: twelve unique stories but containing many similarities.

One obvious similarity is that all are, or were, married to men. They are all straight. This book is not offering an account of LGBTQ+ women's lives – we will respectfully leave others to write such accounts – though we would expect many LGBTQ+ women will find aspects of these twelve stories resonate with their own.

Apart from one story, none of these women's nationality is revealed. It will not, therefore, be clear to the reader where these women were born, raised or now live.

How you interpret these twelve stories will be for you. Every single reader will navigate these accounts in their own unique way – and each way is valid. We have interpreted these stories from our perspective as gender sociologists. You will have your own. These stories have facts but also a lot of interpretation and emotionality, so please don't expect pure objectivity. Simply read and experience, recognise and cultivate whatever lessons work for you and resonate with you.

The way to approach these stories is to view them as individual narratives but to also recognise that each of these women represents in some small or large way, all women.

All women are, therefore, represented in this book. All women's lives are captured in some way in these twelve unique life-history accounts. These stories cut across cultural and national boundaries and all political and religious ideologies.

This reveals an important truth to toxic femininity – it is ubiquitous.

Men are, inevitably, a key element in these women's lives. Within the stories themselves they are a silent presence always performing a role, informing a context, creating a toxic environment or, in a few instances, helping to remove one. Not all the men referred to in these women's lives are toxic or dangerous – though many are.

What is shown to be toxic and dangerous in every story and indeed in the stories of women everywhere, are the historic gender conditions that continue to diminish, restrict, control, determine, endanger and inhibit women from achieving true freedom, true agency and true self-actualisation – limiting their capacity to create for themselves an authentic, pure, safe, positive and independent femininity.

One of the central aims in this book is to expose this toxic gendered condition in women's lives and contribute to eradicating it. Arising from this, with sad if not tragic inevitability, is the most important element in these women's lives, the common thread through each story; the suffering they have undergone. In most cases, this suffering continues in some form or another. In a few cases, it has disappeared.

How has the suffering disappeared? Through the desire for independence of mind and body and the application of self-love.

As one of the women in this book reflects, there are many ways to categorise suffering and you will find in these stories a number of these types. Some of the suffering endured by these women is brutal, dramatic and heart-rending. Some is less dramatic but no less cruelly felt by the woman experiencing it.

Another commonality among these women is that they are all survivors. To be sure, some are thriving more than others, but each of these women is bravely making every effort to maximise her life and to bring happiness and joy into her life and is striving in her own way to overcome often tragic, always desperate, circumstances.

The ultimate goal for each of these women must be self-love and all the precious self-value that accompanies it. Unfortunately, if not inevitably, not all the woman can or will reach this healthy state of identity wellbeing, in which case they will continue to suffer, to be in pain and to live a partial, incomplete life, never finding that personal nirvana, that state of being at peace in oneself. Most of the women in this book are struggling towards self-love. A few have already reached that place. How they reached it and what they had to do, what they had to overcome to do so, is revealed in their stories.

Finally, as authors we apply no critical judgements to any of the women in this book. We know and respect each and every one of them. They are giants, they are lionesses and they are amazing individuals. We've sought to write about them, describe them, with love and care, with empathy and compassion and with understanding. We stand with each of them as they search for happiness, meaning, love and peace in their lives. We stand with all such women, everywhere.

How the Book Is Structured

The book is structured into three parts: Causes, Consequences and The Cure.

Part One – Causes: Introduces the key concepts informing this book; toxic femininity, independent femininity and Totally Inclusive Self-Love, while defining and establishing the circumstances and conditions under which toxic femininity flourishes and is being challenged by women around the world.

Part Two – Consequences: This is sub-divided into three sections:

> *The Overwhelmed Women*
> *(Void and Lost)*
> This opening section explores the lives of two women who have not been able to overcome toxic femininity and are very unlikely to ever do so.

> *The Battling Women*
> *(Shame, Courage, Princess, Poet, Flower, Bird)*
> This section tells of six women currently battling to overcome toxic femininity and create for themselves a healthy, positive life of self-love.

> *The Self-Loving Women*
> *(Alchemist, Heart, Silk, Peace)*
> This final section offers four stories of women who have overcome enormous suffering in life, and in their relationships, to reach a place within themselves of self-love.

Part Three – The Cure: In the final chapter, *Achieving Independence Through Totally Inclusive Self-Love*, we discuss some of the key lessons to be learned from these twelve women and their stories, and reveal how to turn suffering into positive action for a new and better way of being and of living, thereby overcoming and curing toxic femininity.

Chapter Two: Toxic Femininity

At its core, toxic femininity is nothing more than a malign myth – a socially constructed way of thinking about being female and of expressing feminine identity which does women no favours whatsoever, but which suits the mindset of a lot of men through serving to reinforce patriarchal structures, traditional masculinity and associated male privileges. It is only through the persistent perpetuation of these gender myths that toxic femininity can take root in a females' subconscious and subjectivity. But myths can be shattered and the way to do that is by exposing them to critical scrutiny, critical questioning and critical analysis.

This is one aim of this book – to highlight the power of toxic femininity to influence how females think about themselves and conduct their lives, while exposing the myths which enable toxic femininity to flourish.

If you've picked up this book expecting to be told that toxic femininity is the female equivalent of toxic masculinity, then you'll be disappointed. Or more likely relieved. The very idea of equivalence between men's experience of life and women's experience of life is a vast and dangerous over-simplification and not what we claim at all. The aim of this book is to reveal how women experience, express and can overcome toxic femininity and the suffering caused by – for example – shame, depression, tragedy, trauma and acute disenchantment. Also, how the women in this book who triumphed over male-ist discourses and acquired independence of body, spirit and mind, did so through the application of Totally Inclusive Self-Love.

The accounts of these twelve women are real, vivid and frequently painful. They are also regrettably common. For toxic femininity is an insidious, powerful and dangerous virus. As a socially discursive condition, it can readily materialise as both language and practice – it takes root in a woman's subjectivity and sense of feminine self and can remain there for a lifetime. It can come to define a woman, circumscribe her potential and reduce her agency. Its biggest risk to women lies in its apparent benignity and normalisation of women and their femininity as passive, docile, subservient, shameful and needy of men.

Toxic Genders

What this tells us is that gender identity is not neutral – it is political. It is made political by the power of an historic gender order and associated culture, one which has privileged hegemonic masculinity (aka toxic masculinity) over more liberal and progressive forms of male identity. Accepting the multiplicity of masculinities, it remains the case that hegemonic masculinity continues to dominate the lives and subjectivities of a large number of men, perhaps the vast majority of men, even as we move through the twenty-first century.

So how do we define hegemonic (toxic) masculinity?

> *Hegemonic (toxic) masculinity is a form of male behaviour and expression of male identity that seeks to reinforce men's power and patriarchal values. Based on characteristics such as competition, ambition, self-reliance, physical strength, aggression and homophobia, the image that is perpetrated celebrates physical toughness, the endurance of hardships, aggressiveness, a rugged heterosexuality, and unemotional logic.*

Whitehead, 2021

The power of hegemonic masculinity lies in its persuasiveness as a dominant, apparently 'natural' way of being a man. This is offered as a 'truth' to men and to women, and in so doing conceals its ideological constitution. Yet there is nothing natural nor inevitable about this masculinity – it is entirely and always a socially constructed version of male identity, one intended to perpetuate a gender order which places (straight) men at the top of any social/political/economic hierarchy.

For sociologists and psychologists, none of this is particularly new – more than five decades of global academic research into men and masculinities has exposed the impact of hegemonic (toxic) masculinity on the lives of women and men of all nationalities, classes, races, ethnicities, sexualities, religions and social groupings. No longer are men and masculinities invisible in the way they were, say, in the 1970s before feminist theorists began to look more closely at the identity constructs of men and the multiplicity of masculinities. This burgeoning critical analysis was reinforced in 2019 with the American Psychological Association's publication of a 36-page report detailing the danger that traditional (hegemonic) masculinity poses to men's mental health and general wellbeing. From being the province of a small number of gender sociologists, the critical study of men and masculinities has now expanded to a global mainstream audience, with all sexes increasingly concerned to look more closely at the circumstances under which males become men and masculinities are performed. Since 2006 and the global rise of the #MeToo movement, this focus has assumed greater urgency not least due to the realisation that progressive society needs to better understand male identity dynamics if it is ever to challenge and overturn rape culture, men's violence, misogyny and institutionalised sexism.

Consequently, there is today a lot of noise around men – their similarities, differences and their problems – which is in stark and revealing contrast to the deadening silence which surrounded men and their masculinities for all the millennia previous.

At long last, men are under a critical global spotlight. To be sure, this is creating much angst, anger, malaise and resistance amongst a lot of men, but it is also creating something much more positive and hopeful – self-aware liberal men with a progressive masculine identity (Whitehead, 2021).

Nevertheless, one big question remains; how does hegemonic/toxic masculinity impact on women's subjectivities? Because it surely must. It would be inconceivable that women's own sense of feminine self has not been adversely influenced by millennia of hegemonic masculine behaviour in men and the persistent messaging that females are inferior to males.

In the research we've undertaken, the consequence is revealed to be patriarchal-defined feminine gender identity association, or toxic femininity for short.

> *Patriarchal-defined feminine gender identity association, or toxic femininity, is the internalisation and expression of negative, painful feelings and emotions produced by shame, guilt, rejection, frustration, neglect, confusion, disenchantment, abuse, violence and hopelessness. Toxic femininity is a mindset of helplessness, a belief that one is no longer worthy of love or of value; a state of being wherein the woman presents her self only for the judgement and consumption of men and others, not for her innate well-being. Underpinning and reinforcing toxic femininity are the myths of traditional feminine identity which posit women as naturally needy, emotional and secondary to males.*

For toxic femininity to be an effective vehicle for male hegemony it must move from myth to reality. That is, whatever gender myths – operating as codes, messages, stereotypes, beliefs and thinking – exist in society they must be powerful and persuasive enough to create related behaviour patterns in individuals. For it is not through violence and its threat alone that toxic femininity is enabled; it is through females believing in the myths and subsequently acting them out in their daily lives, effectively creating reality from the myths.

From Myths to Reality

Toxic femininity arises when women realise their aspirations and expectations as a woman are impossible to achieve – being in direct conflict with their lived reality – resulting in depression and dejection. It arises when women succumb to self-blame, sometimes self-harm, when a relationship goes bad or when their partner is unfaithful, violent, abusive or just emotionally absent. It arises when women, conditioned to search for and find the perfect love, the pure relationship, instead find rejection, pain, misunderstanding and loneliness. And it arises when a woman cannot comprehend nor tolerate the state of her life, and therefore becomes overwhelmed by regret, confusion, frustration, bitterness, even self-loathing. If a woman believes she can only be fully validated as a person when she is loved by a man, then that is a very dangerous assumption because not only is she risking all for a man, but when such relationships end the woman takes it as personal failure, a diminishing of her worth as a woman, a rejection of her femininity. She loses her sense of self.

Toxic femininity can arise in women who strive to be perfect in every way (physically and in their relationships) but then find such perfection impossible to achieve; attempting to reach this pinnacle of 'female perfection' is ultimately a hopeless, futile self-destructive quest. It will arise in those women who, consciously or not, end up existing only to please men. Toxic femininity can arise in younger women who believe their value can only be measured through a high-profile but ultimately amorphous social media presence – a virtual validation through 'likes' – and/or through collaborating in a masculine culture which sexually objectifies females. It can arise in women who constantly yearn for an approving male gaze and approbation, and are tempted to try and behave like men, to join the 'boys club', in order to receive such approval. Toxic femininity is not mediated by wealth, prestige or social status. Any woman who externalises her sense of worth onto the perception of others (husband, family, friends, bosses) and requires validation from others in order to feel of value, is at risk.

Toxic femininity is the noxious, always dangerous, potentially lethal condition which takes root in a woman when she fails to recognise her true value as a woman, as a human being; and especially when she uncritically adheres to gender rules and regulations requiring she conform to traditional feminine values – mostly to suit men. In other words, when she is no longer living an authentic life – her life.

Toxic femininity is in those women who are not living for themselves but for others, especially male lovers and partners. And it is in those women who, frustrated and despairing of their own life, their lack of agency, turn on other women with anger, aggression and negative judgement.

An extreme example of toxic femininity in action would be when women force young girls to undergo female genital mutilation. Whether they do so from the misguided belief that this is somehow of benefit to these young girls once they become women, or fulfils a dominant religious/cultural code, the result it the same; females colluding in the male-ist oppression of other females.

As with female genital mutilation, toxic femininity is not a new condition for women. It has always been a dominant condition for women. Most women today, and through history, have experience of toxic femininity. It will come to a woman no matter her class, sexuality, nationality, religion, education or culture. It is almost unavoidable; particularly for those women who invest their whole sense of worth and validation in romantic love and the approving gaze of others – especially male lovers and partners.

Unlike toxic masculinity in men, toxic femininity in women is not expressed through dysfunctional emotional intelligence invariably arising from an incessant quest for power, control and dominance. Rather, toxic femininity is a by-product of toxic masculinity – it is the poison which arises in women's bodies and minds when they experience not just the pain of lost love, but the hopelessness of trying to be perfect, not for themselves but for men who ultimately neither understand nor value them.

Women are generally recognised to be emotionally intelligent, empathetic individuals. It is how they are raised; perhaps it is what they are born with. But that emotionality becomes toxic when women internalise the negative judgements of others and conclude that they are worthless, disposable failures. That emotionality, originally a precious gift, becomes toxic when a woman, knowingly or not, treats other women in a toxic manner; thereby cascading toxic femininity onto other females through abusive and aggressive behaviour, negative judgement and pressure to conform to gender stereotypes.

This book shows how women can reject toxic femininity and the gendered, idealised, unachievable notions of perfection which inevitably accompany it, and instead embrace their authentic selves. It gives real-life examples of women doing precisely this.

Despite the progress being made in many areas of gender equity, countless numbers of women around the world remain trapped by unrealistic expectations, and familial and societal pressures which are themselves a direct consequence of traditional gender values and toxic male attitudes. Women are at risk of internalising any failure to meet these expectations of 'perfection' as their personal failure when in fact it is societal values that are the cause, underpinned by traditional (toxic) masculine behaviours.

As with masculinity, femininity is multiple. And as we reveal in the next chapter, toxic femininity is certainly not the only femininity available to women/females. However, toxic femininity is the feminine identity that has historically been presented to and imposed upon females around the world as the most desirable and 'normal' way of being a woman, in which case we can identify it has having hegemonic properties. In other words, it becomes the hegemonic femininity.

Much as it might suit many men to claim otherwise, hegemonic/toxic femininity is neither desirable nor a biologically/psychologically 'normal' state for women. It is nothing more or less than a male-ist, ideologically constituted femininity, infused with gender myths designed to fit women into a patriarchal system for the benefit of men.

More research certainly needs to be undertaken into patriarchal-defined feminine gender identity association (hegemonic femininity/toxic femininity) and its impact on women's lives and subjectivities. Such research would be a valuable counter to the dominance of this feminine identity while encouraging women to reject any way of being feminine which ultimately results in their submission to a patriarchal gender order and thereby lessens their sense of female agency.

Whatever research into femininities is undertaken, it is very likely to highlight alternative ways of being female and a woman – ways not invested in traditional gender values. For there are and always will be multiple femininities and therefore multiple ways of expressing a feminine sense of self. One of these ways, or femininities, is an especially important counter to toxic femininity: we name it independent femininity.

Chapter Three: Independent Femininity

The social and cultural discourses informing male and female identities have always been subject to change – that is an historical fact. But what is also an historical fact is that never in human history have gender discourses changed so profoundly and so quickly as they have since the end of the Second World War.

The beginnings of what is now a full-blooded gender revolution were first spotted by American sociologists such as Joseph Pleck and Ruth Hartley in the 1950s. They warned of an emergent 'trauma in male socialisation' processes resulting from dramatically changing familial/work circumstances, new gender/sex roles, the inflexibility of gender stereotypes and the limitations of previously dominant male gender role models (see Whitehead, 2025b for elaboration; also, Whitehead 2002).

These and related indicators (i.e. globalisation and the massification of higher education), suggested the post-war world would be a very different place for gender/sexual relationships than previously and at the forefront of this transformation were the heightened expectations of women. In other words, traditional gender identities were being replaced by something altogether more liberating, at least for females. For males, not much changed – at least at first. Over the subsequent decades most men continued through life unaware of, or choosing to ignore, the fact that women were undergoing a dramatic shift in their feminine consciousness. Eventually, however, men would have to wake up to the new revolution; which is where we are at today – with men more awake to, though not all welcoming of, the new gender reality.

But to make this revolution work, women would first have to reject and overcome all those centuries of traditional gender thinking around feminine identity and to do that they would need agency – the desire, opportunity and capacity to act and think for oneself.

Agency

One key ingredient in toxic femininity is its removal or diminishment of agency. That is, the female fails to recognise the conditions of her own oppression or if she does, she feels unable to overcome them.

To take a current example; would women in Afghanistan, subjected as they are to the gender apartheid regime of the Taliban, be suffering from toxic femininity? The answer would be, only those women who align themselves with the Taliban dictatorship and consider the gender repressions of such to be natural, justified and acceptable. In other words, knowingly or not, they actively collaborate and collude in the oppression of themselves and other women.

Afghan women who silently or actively resist would not be suffering from toxic femininity, for they are not confused by, mistaken as to, or unaware of, their reduced state. Though one needs to recognise that to try and live under such a terrible gender apartheid requires not just emotional and mental resilience of the highest order, but infinite patience reinforced by a belief that things will, eventually, get better. In short, the women need to have hope.

And what does that hope look like?

In our opinion, any hope must be invested with agency – that is, the women yearn and strive to become independent thinkers, actors, individuals. They may well still want men in their lives – as fathers, sons, brothers, lovers, husbands – but what they don't want and will not tolerate is being reduced to slavery-like conditions in order to appease the toxic masculine identities of men.

What can be said of Afghan women living under the Taliban regime of gender apartheid is equally true of any women living anywhere under the control of men, patriarchal discourses and traditional gender values and who do so because they have neither the material power and resources nor the emotional self-awareness to change their dire circumstances.

This is why we describe this alternative femininity as independent; that is, enlightened, self-aware, agentic and self-actualising. Simply put, it is being and living as a free woman. All these descriptors point towards a much healthier way of being a woman and of expressing feminine identity. The reason it is healthier is because independent femininity does not reduce the woman to a component in a male-dominated social machine.

Independent femininity is a truly authentic femininity – one created through the agency and self-awareness of the woman. It is not imposed on the woman through laws, culture, violence, oppression, threat, coercion and propaganda.

So here we have a classic gender identity binary. On the one side are the traditional: those women who continue to believe that they need a man in order to thrive, survive and validate their sense of womanhood and place in the world. On the other side are the independent: those who are quite happy pursuing their own life journey with or without a male partner in tow.

While it will be true that there has always been this prevailing binary in women's subjectivity and sense of self, what we are witnessing today is at least a global evolution in core femininity, if not a global revolution. And some of the evidence for this revolution is contained in two prominent, overlapping and self-sustaining trends – singletons and celibacy.

Growing Apart

Globally, there are now over two billion single people and the number is rising fast. Look at the demographics of most any country and one fact becomes apparent – women and men are not getting married; growing numbers are not even living together.

Across the world, younger generations are defying traditional social norms and deciding on solo living. In China the singles population reached a record 239 million in 2021 with more than half of Chinese aged twenty-five to twenty-nine now living solo lives. In the USA, 46.4% of the adult population are single, up from just 22% in 1950. The UK has seen singletons rise to 30% of all households, 8.4 million people. A staggering 42% of all households in South Korea are now single-person, with over half of all men in their thirties living solo lives. The condition of singleton lifestyles is now so common in Japan that they've produced a name for it: ohitorisama; meaning 'living alone' and 'going solo'. Even countries with a traditionally strong marriage culture, such as Thailand, Saudi Arabia, Vietnam, Nigeria, India and Pakistan, are seeing a rise in singletons. It is an unstoppable trend, cutting across class, religious, racial and ethnic lines (see Whitehead, 2024a).

With a quarter of the world's population and about a third of all people over fifteen years of age living single lives, the 'super solo' society is well and truly with us. Yet while that leaves singles with plenty of choice, not many of them seem keen to hitch up anytime soon and certainly not in order to reproduce. Because another global trend is aligning with the rise in singletons and that is celibacy.

The rise of voluntary celibates has been evident in Japan and South Korea for over a decade, though now we are seeing it expand worldwide.

In January 2024, Google reported a 90% increase in searches for celibacy in the UK, while the #celibacy hashtag on TikTok has had more than 195 million views with many voluntary celibates claiming it improves their mental health and sense of wellbeing. In the US, voluntary celibacy has been on the rise for several years. In 2021, the General Social Survey found that 25% of Americans over the age of eighteen hadn't had sex once in the previous twelve months – a thirty-year high. Identical shifts in sexual behaviour are apparent around the world, including China, New Zealand, even that most romantic of countries, France (see Whitehead, 2024a).

Without doubt, celibacy is having a cultural moment, though perhaps it is here to stay, for as Dr Justin Lehmiller of the Sex and Psychology Podcast, states:

> *"There is a long-term trend among people, today, in general, for having less sex with few partners. Humans are increasingly less sexually active, with some foregoing sex altogether."*
>
> Whitehead, 2024a

The reason for the rise in solo living, decline in marriage, rise in celibacy and the corresponding decline in births, is not simply because of economic pressures arising from urbanised living – most of us are far better off than our ancestors while – as governments such as China and Japan are realising – if women are determined not to get married and have children then offering them financial incentives won't get them to change their minds.

No, the reason for these dramatic and far-reaching changes is primarily to do with choice and culture.

The choice is being made by women to not get married. As the evidence shows, increasing numbers of women are not even dating. Many are living celibate lives, perhaps interspersed by occasional and relatively brief,sexual relations.

The culture is a celebration of individualism – the right of the individual to pursue their happiness and dreams independent of societal expectations surrounding gender and sexual behaviour.

This is women deciding for themselves just what type of life they intend to have and who, if anyone, they will accept to accompany them on their journey. If increasing numbers of women decide to make that a solo voyage then that is an entirely legitimate expression of their independent femininity.

There is also a third trend in women's relationships which corresponds with independent femininity, and that is the increase in the number of women experiencing same-sex relationships.

Research in the USA reveals that women are now almost three-times more likely to report same-sex intimacy as men, with 7% self-defining as gay compared to 4% of men. Similarly, three times as many women than men identify as bisexual (Dotinga, 2016). In the UK, a 2021 study found that between 2011 and 2019, college-age women increasingly moved away from exclusive heterosexuality. In 2019, 65% of women reported only being attracted to men, a noticeable decrease from 77% in 2011 (Klein, 2021).

All of this suggests that independent femininity accompanies a more fluid interpretation and expression of sexuality, with women's orientations becoming less rigid than men's.

However, with a majority of men globally still drawn towards traditional/ hegemonic presentations of masculinity, along with the homophobia and transphobia this engenders, indicates a distancing between a progressive femininity and a regressive masculinity; a claim supported by global research revealing a widening 'Gen Z gender ideological gap' between liberal women and conservative men. As John Burnham-Murdoch (2024) reports:

> *"In countries on every continent, an ideological gap has opened up between young men and women. Tens of millions of people who occupy the same cities, workplaces, classrooms and even homes, no longer see eye to eye...Today's under-thirties are undergoing a great gender divergence."*

As any agentic individual must, increasing numbers of women are aspiring to a more self-created identity, one not bound up in rigid gender thinking and expectations (Whitehead, 2025). Such women are rejecting the historic gender conditions that determined they could only achieve a socially acceptable feminine identity by getting married, having children and by investing their sense of femaleness in compulsory heterosexuality and the approving gaze of others.

For sure, one can interpret the rise in singleton lifestyles, voluntary celibacy and bisexuality in a number of ways – after all, these are complex and dynamic social phenomena – but what cannot be misinterpreted is their impact on traditional gender norms and, in particular, on traditional/toxic femininity. Whatever one's analysis, the outcome is unmistakable, which is that increasing numbers of women are rejecting traditional gender values, a traditional gender/sex role identity and striking out for independent living. For many women that will still mean marriage, children and heterosexual family life but for a great many more it will mean creating their own solo lifestyle.

The gender identity changes forecast by sociologists over seventy years ago are now with us in full-force and there is no power on earth which can stop them and put women back in their patriarchal box.

However, this trend towards independent femininity cannot take place without emotional resilience and a strong sense of self. Whatever our gender, if we are to express true agentic independence of mind and body we must draw on our emotional reserves. That is, we must first believe we are worthy of being independent while also brave and strong enough to carry the consequences of independent thinking and action. As we reveal in this book, such agentic action first requires self-love.

In our judgement, the rise of singleton lifestyles coupled with celibacy and non-exclusive heterosexuality, while not suiting governments or indeed many men, is a demonstration of feminine independence. It is an almost inevitable consequence of women rejecting millennia without agency and choice over their lifestyles, futures and options. <u>This is not to suggest that all women are happy or satisfied with this situation</u>. No doubt a great many straight women would dearly love to have a male partner in their lives, someone with whom they can share their future on a fair, equitable and healthy basis. In which case, the fact that these women are living solo, celibate and in many cases, bisexual lives, says more about the suitability of men as safe and reliable partners than it does about women.

Importantly, it confirms that women have changed while men still have some catching up to do, leaving societies around the world facing not just a decline in marriages and birth rates but a growing separation of the sexes.

In short, women and men are not just living apart; they are increasingly growing apart.

However, as the women in this book reveal about themselves, whether living with a man or living a solo life, in the end one must find within oneself that nugget of self-love. For without this there can be little chance of ever moving to a place of independent, healthy self-awareness; a way of life and being which rejects all the social pressure placed on women to invest their identity and validity in male-ist dictates and in the approving judgements of men.

Chapter Four: Totally Inclusive Self-Love

A woman with toxic femininity may well ask: "who will love me?"
A woman with independent femininity will always answer: "I love me".

As you will have gathered, our case for independent femininity and against toxic femininity contains a particular piece of evidence – self-love. Without this, no individual can live a truly fulfilling and agentic life. It is fundamental to peace of mind, a calm spirit, a sense of worth, value and validation. To be truly independent in mind, body and spirit one needs to first love one's self, otherwise that independent journey of self-creation cannot even begin (Whitehead, 2025).

In short, to overcome the myths of toxic femininity a female must first believe she is worth more than the myths tell her she is.

That said, the term 'self-love' comes laden with assumptions, misunderstandings and baggage. Indeed, rarely has a single word or concept caused more confusion than this one. Go to almost any dictionary, from Oxford downwards, and you'll find self-love listed up there along with negative traits such as vanity, egotism, boastfulness, arrogance and selfishness.

This is not what self-love is. Self-love is healthy; it is essential that every human being has it; it is a vital element in well-being; it can literally be a life-saver.

At the same time, it is important to note that there are different types and expressions of self-love: it can be partial (relying on the validation of others); it can be selfish (driven by ego and overweening self-regard); and it can be inclusive (totally self-aware).

The definition we are using and aim to promote in this book is Totally Inclusive Self-Love, defined as follows:

> Totally Inclusive Self-Love means understanding oneself, valuing oneself, nurturing oneself, protecting oneself, empowering oneself, thereby ensuring one is able to grow in a self-aware and contented state. It also means accepting one's strengths and weaknesses together with the components that constitute one's intersectional identity.

That definition is not partial nor is it selfish, the reason being, that one cannot achieve Totally Inclusive Self-Love without first accepting the inclusive character of all identities, all communities, all societies and all individuals. Totally Inclusive Self-Love entitles you to protect yourself, nurture yourself, create yourself, and live an independent life even when surrounded by loved ones and friends. What it doesn't allow is this healthy need for self-actualisation and agentic living to become corrupted through anger, hatred, discrimination, division and unhealthy selfishness. In other words, the inclusivity element means just that – inclusivity toward everyone (see Whitehead, 2022).

You will have spotted in the above definition a particular term – intersectional. This deserves some explanation.

> 'Intersectionality recognises that each individual identity exists at the intersections of many aspects of self and social power. It encourages the recognition that gender intersects with, for example, race, sex, sexuality, ability, ethnicity, age, culture and class to produce the individual. As discrete forms of oppression, these variables combine to have a powerful impact on women's lives and in ways which are not always apparent to the individual.'
>
> Whitehead et al, 2014; also Hill Collins & Bilge, 2020

Every individual on earth, now or who has ever lived, has an intersectional identity; that is, components which together serve to constitute the individual. These components will include gender, sex, sexuality, race, nationality, ethnicity, religion, spirituality, age, ability, class, career, marital/relationship status and familial status.

To achieve Totally Inclusive Self-Love, you must first accept all the components which make up you. Some of these you will be able to change (i.e. professional identity); others you won't be able to change (i.e. sexuality).

Similarly, some of the components will be more oppressive and restrictive than others, notably those around gender, race and ethnicity. Some will be hard work to achieve but potentially liberating (i.e. education). Others will be firmly placed within your particular comfort zone. And a few you may not even recognise until you stop to think about it.

What this tells us is that firstly, no two people are totally alike and secondly, that if we cannot recognise who we are, then we cannot begin to change the bits we need to.

So only you can achieve Totally Inclusive Self-Love, because only you know who and what you really are. For women, this has profound implications.

Historically, and as we see in the gender apartheid regimes which exist in the world today, women have been told who they must be and how they must be in order to deserve love, protection and acceptance – inevitably from men.

The message is always – do as I want, as we men want, and all will be well – 'misbehave' and there will be consequences.

And consequences there often are, with women around the world subjected to male violence, discrimination and misogyny, not just in the home but in the street, organisations, social media and in countless numbers of judicial, social, corporate and private spaces.

This is how toxic femininity acts to pressure women to conform to the rule of men – by coercion and intimidation reinforced through the social/political discourses and myths of 'natural gender differences'.

External intimidation of women by men is fairly easy to spot, though not always easy to stop. However, it is when that external intimidation becomes internalised that the real problems arise for women.

Again, to use the example of Afghan women; they cannot easily physically challenge the gender apartheid that exists around them but they can at least recognise it – it is explicit and unapologetic. This physical threat is, of course, a great danger to these women. But the greater danger is when they accept the misogyny as normal. Once any woman has accepted her reduced position in society (or in a family, community, organisation) as normal and justified so has she internalised that oppression and made it a key part of her identity as a woman. She has become her own oppressor, colluding unwittingly in her own subjugation.

Once this happens, it becomes much harder to acquire Totally Inclusive Self-Love. As you will see from the twelve women in this book, those who overcame toxic femininity could only do so by first recognising its insidious presence in their lives – by reflecting and acting against those external and internal behaviours, attitudes, assumptions, threats and fears which served to maintain the woman in a place of pain and suffering. Having woken up to the conditions which hitherto constrained them, so these women were in a position to act; to advance to an independent mindset if not always to being single and living solo lives.

This is an important point to stress – Totally Inclusive Self-Love does not require any individual to live a solo-life. That may well be the best outcome for many women, but it is not a prerequisite.

Simply, Totally Inclusive Self-Love arises when a woman stops attempting to achieve self-validation by striving to meet the expectations of others and gaining the love of others and instead finds her true worth, identity, validation and trust in loving herself, forgiving herself and understanding herself.

Once a woman loves herself, then toxic femininity cannot take root within her.

Is this process of removing toxic femininity difficult and fraught? No. Once a woman has recognised the root cause of her anxiety, the mind-state and conditions which have brought about her pain, then she has begun the journey to a guilt-free, non-toxic, powerful, highly positive feminine identity and sense of self. This moment of turning away from toxic femininity and the values it carries, is for such women a joyful one, full of hope, release, empowerment and fun. There is unbounded delight in finally rejecting the narrative of toxicity and in embracing a newly emergent and stronger feminine self.

All of this sounds eminently healthy both for mind and body. So why is self-love often looked upon negatively, a little bit OTT? To answer that question let us clarify what Totally Inclusive Self-Love is NOT.

- It is not narcissism. It is not vanity or self-adulation, nor is it always believing one is right.

- It is not a power-play. It is not an obsession with one's own position, authority, status, dominance or need to control others.

- It is not self-obsession. It is not disregarding or being uncaring of the needs of others, being inconsiderate, nor being self-absorbed to the point where one has no empathy for others.

- It is not ego-mania. It is not obsessive self-regarding to the extent of excluding anyone else's ego, nor seeking to diminish anyone else's self-worth in order to feel good.

- It is not introversion. It is not retreating so far into one's self that one becomes a recluse.

- It is not weakness. It can only be acquired through balance, determination, resolve and patience.

- It is not emotional dysfunctionality. On the contrary, to acquire self-love one must develop emotional intelligence. Self-love requires empathy, sympathy, forgiveness, understanding – and a touch of wisdom.

- It is not being perfect: perfection within oneself is never achievable and anyone with self-love knows this. They know their weaknesses, indeed they appreciate their weaknesses as much as they appreciate their strengths.

Is Totally Inclusive Self-Love selfish? Yes, to the extent that selfishness is not always and inevitably bad. Totally Inclusive Self-Love is <u>healthy selfishness</u>, where the individual makes decisions not based on the persuasiveness, demands or expectations of others, but on their own safety, protection, wellbeing and needs.

Whatever humans do in their lives, whatever decisions they make, there invariably lies behind those actions and decisions a desire for happiness, for contentment and for satisfaction. But you cannot achieve sustainable happiness without self-love. You cannot achieve real contentment without self-love. And you'll never be satisfied with your life if you are not content within your self.

Searching for self-love is not a narcissistic ego-trip; it is an essential journey that every woman, every human being, should be brave and confident enough to undertake.

The journey towards Totally Inclusive Self-Love begins with **self-awareness**: being reflective, emotionally aware, recognising one's flow of emotions, feelings, patterns, tendencies and values.

This enables **self-validation** and **self-expression**, two supporting aspects of identity. Both allow the individual to assert themselves in a liberating, self-actualising way.

But self-love cannot function fully unless the individual cares for herself. Therefore, **self-care** and **self-protection** become actions of care which that individual must perform on her own behalf – not rely on others to do it for her.

The next stage is **self-sufficiency** and **self-independence**. Here, the individual is aware of her strengths and weaknesses and has accepted them, forgiven herself for having those weaknesses, recognised them as core elements of herself, and can live with these traits in a healthy, mindful, state. The individual is whole within herself, not full of emotional vacuums needing to be filled by others.

Finally, the individual reaches a stage of **self-management** and **self-development**. At this point a woman, for example, is feeling complete within herself; she trusts her self and in her own judgements; she is able to love others unconditionally but not to the extent of jeopardising her own well-being. The individual continues to progress and to develop greater emotional intelligence, acquiring better understanding of how other people may be struggling with various forms of toxicity.

When an individual reaches this final level, she will be emotionally resilient, of a calm mind, strongly empathetic and mentally healthy. Her physical state will benefit also. Totally Inclusive Self-Love creates circumstances wherein a person is enveloped by both inner and outer-love.

A person with Totally Inclusive Self-Love can connect with others in a positive and healthy way. She will have the empathy to do so. A person with Totally Inclusive Self-Love will give and receive love much more readily. She will be open to love not least because she can better cope with the insecurities and anxieties that accompany emotional openness and emotional exposure.

In the ultimate state of Totally Inclusive Self-Love, a person loves every single aspect of her or himself. It is unconditional love for oneself. Such love is a state of mind, a way of relating to the world around you. It is not contingent on achieving wealth, power, material success or being loved in return. It is never partial; it is inevitably and necessarily fully and totally inclusive of all aspects of oneself.

At the beginning of this chapter we recognised the complexity and diversity among women, but also the similarities. When a woman is embracing Totally Inclusive Self-Love, she will still be a unique individual, true to herself, but she will also be able to recognise how similar she is to other women. She will be able to love other women not as rivals but as extensions of herself. We are all connected and Totally Inclusive Self-Love is a most powerful way of recognising and strengthening that connection.

In other words, self-love is not just about the self, the individual. Ultimately it is about the whole; all of us as a global society.

The journey towards Totally Inclusive Self-Love is, for all women and men, a journey of healing. It is a way of ameliorating pain, anguish, despair, depression and self-loathing. It is also a form of protection. And the most effective and complete level of protection arises when a woman recognises and accepts all aspects of herself – her desires, her needs, her hopes, her fears and her insecurities.

The healthiest emotional condition for any individual is achieved when that person embraces all facets of their intersectional identity; when they are being truly authentic and no longer acting out roles and behaviours for social convention or in order to appease others or to acquire the approval and approbation of others. When one is able to embrace all facets of oneself, one is able to better accept all facets of others.

Therein arises the state of Totally Inclusive Self-Love.

Every woman on earth, indeed every individual, is a mixture of elements that in dynamic fashion serve to create the sense of wholeness – the identity. We should not seek to negate or deny, marginalise or reduce, any identity element within ourselves. Nor should we do the same to others.

Totally Inclusive Self-Love is, in essence, action. It is action to change the whole by changing the self, the individual. Not in any idealistic or unhealthy way, nor for any corrosive or corrupting reason, but solely for goodness, joy and wellbeing – for everyone's benefit.

Thus arises the solution to toxic femininity.

Totally Inclusive Self-Love – self-love that recognises and welcomes all facets of one's identity – is the only and most powerful antidote to toxic femininity. Indeed, it is the most powerful antidote to all toxicities that infect the human condition.

If we love ourselves unconditionally and do so full of love for the world around us, we cannot foster toxicity, we cannot succumb to self-loathing, we cannot retreat to hatred and violence, and we certainly cannot deny that we are each of us worthy of love – for we are each the ones who make the whole.

Part Two: Consequences

1: The Overwhelmed Women

Chapter Five: Void

LONE BIRD IN THE SKY

Childhood memories are at best, selective. Certain days, people and moments stay vivid, though most are lost in time. Yet while our memory will fade and even misinform us, our experiences of childhood are never fully absent. These early circumstances of life are etched in us, in our selves. They have formed us; created the mould into which the individual essence gets poured and then hardens over time.

Void was only six months old when her newly widowed father, exasperated by her crying and disgusted at her persistent skin infection, rejected her. He did so very clearly and quite deliberately. He took his baby daughter out into the cold autumn yard, placed her down on the stone floor and walked back into his house, shutting the door behind him. There Void lay for several hours; while the farm dogs sniffed her swathed body, the crows hovered above, and she wailed. Until an alarmed neighbour picked her up and took her in. Seventy-eight years later that moment remains pivotal in Void's life journey. She knows it happened because her grandmother told her so. But while Void cannot recall the day her father rejected her, she can never erase her childhood experiences, nor her life thereafter. What she has had to contend with as a woman is carved in her deeply wrinkled, sun-burnt, grim and deeply pessimistic face. A face of someone who has experienced suffering, loneliness and abuse.

Where does the toxicity begin? Does it begin early in a life, or in the lives which beget that life? Her father was violent, quick-tempered, but suffering too. He was poor in a poor country. He had little where having little meant living on the edge of existence. But he had enough of something to attract a second wife and sire three more children.

While her father grew another family, Void withered, rejected not only by her father but subsequently by her stepmother. Only her grandmother supported her – in effect saving her life.

Void was an outcast in her own family, discarded by the one person who should have loved her unconditionally – her father. She never knew her mother. She never experienced positive and compassionate femininity. She grew accustomed to acute solitariness in her soul, even while surrounded by other human beings.

But can any father fully replace a lost mother? Can any child, especially a girl, grow to adult wellbeing without ever knowing the warmth and security of their mother? For millions of people these are not rhetorical questions but real ones; questions that perhaps never get fully answered in any life.

Void never tried to answer those questions for herself because to even attempt to do so would open up old wounds, expose the scars and cause regret. And regret can be a canker in the soul; it can fester as the years pass by along with any opportunities. Much healthier, and safer, to accept the realities of life, even if the pain of living is at times unbearable.

Pain or not, Void survived. She went on to have her own husband and family – four children, eight grandchildren. But she also created a legacy of toxicity, a toxic femininity which she never could erase within herself and which at seventy-eight years of age she is now condemned to die with.

Survival

When an animal is cast out from the group it must quickly learn to survive or it will die. And it is no different for a human. Void grew an armour to protect her from the vicissitudes of life; her poverty, her loneliness, her sense of isolation, the abuse of men and the condemnation of other women. She grew strong, but at a price. Her defence against defeatism was determination. Her defence against sadness was to have no self-pity. Her defence against emotional trauma was to have no emotions – at least not visible ones.

Her defence against unrealised hope was to have none. Life has not been hard on Void, at least in her own mind. Starting from her father and percolating down through all of her familial relationships is the belief that no one will be kind to her, no one will give her love and no one will truly care. That is just a fact of life.

> "How many nights have I cried myself to sleep? I don't know. Too many. But this is life. We must not expect anything because we'll just be disappointed. I cannot be disappointed any more."

The price she paid for these defences was toxic femininity. It emerged as emotional cruelty to her own children and continued through their own marriages, with her playing the role of the sour and poisonous mother-in-law.

The toxicity she caused was, in Void's eyes, not toxicity at all but simply how women must be if they were to survive, be strong in a world dominated by abusive and potentially violent men. Void grew to be intolerant of others, resentful, coarse, quick to anger, greedy for material security and selfish. Her sharp tongue and judgemental attitude were especially turned towards those women who wanted something different, something better for themselves, who rejected the constraints of traditional womanhood.

Void's children rarely experienced a kind word from her, and never a warm hug and kiss. They grew up in an emotionally cold and sterile environment, where one wrong word could result in a beating from either parent.

Look into the eyes of Void and you see decades of pain, hardship, isolation and unhappiness. Yet this is not a physically weak woman. In her seventies she was still growing produce and selling it to the local community, though today she is largely incapacitated through a stroke.

Where Void is weak is in her lack of self-understanding. This is not a woman who has indulged in much self-reflection. But then, did she have the resources for such analysis? Void left school aged eleven and has lived all her life in a community burdened by traditional gender values enacted in an unforgiving political and economic environment. It is no surprise, therefore, that her sense of worth as a woman is conditioned on the value men place on her.

> *"Women are born to be submissive to men. It is their destiny. If a woman is not submissive to her husband then she can expect to be treated badly by him."*

Submission can take many forms but for Void it was irrevocably connected to survival. She learned to be a silent loser in her marriage because that way she kept her husband. To become a divorced mother of four meant total destitution. She would lose everything. She had no one to help her, so leaving her husband was not an option. Void's own self-esteem and happiness came to matter less to her than her husband's masculine pride. Void never allowed any maternal and empathetic femininity to surface for fear of it becoming a weakness, a chip in her armour.

All her life, Void had one aim – to survive and if this meant negating her self-expression, denying her own right to exist as an independent woman and reducing her agency, then that was a small price to pay – so she reasoned.

Love

In the absence of tenderness and care, can love flourish? Indeed, can it even exist? For Void, love is not a word that comes easily to her lips.

> *"Love? What do you mean by that? I have loved all my children and when I was first married I loved my husband. But life changes us. Love is best kept to romantic novels. It is not life."*

One of the most natural impulses of any child, if not any adult, is to desire love. To be wanted, to be cared for and to belong. Void certainly belonged, first to her father's new family and then to her husband, whom she met aged seventeen and married a year later, pregnant with their first child. But it was a caged belonging, promising only a love that was conditional. The men she wanted to love her demanded she first yield to them before they gave her their love: love that came with threats attached, love that quickly excluded if she did not accept the conditions. The main condition of such love is always submission to male authority.

Like many emotionally traumatised young women, Void went from one dominating male abuser (her father) to another (her husband), a seamless link that took her further and further away from her own possibility of self-actualisation.

During the first ten years of marriage, Void gave birth to four children. Her husband played no role in their upbringing. As he saw it, that was a 'woman's job'. And Void agreed. She never questioned the gender status quo imposed on her by her family and her community. But while her husband became serially unfaithful and spent his evenings drinking in bars, Void grew coarser, less attractive and less desirable to any man. At least this meant she could get more sleep and not have to succumb to her husband's crude advances usually made in a drunken stupor.

Void's vulgar and uncultured behaviour may have saved her from unwanted sex but it did not go down well with her husband. He beat her.

> *"I remember one beating very well. We were attending a friend's wedding in the village. Lots of people were attending. I was eating the meal when suddenly my husband got up from the table and slapped me hard across the face. Then he picked up his shoe and started hitting me with that. The other guests had to stop him. I was badly bruised but no one helped me. In those days it was considered normal for a husband to beat his wife. Why did he beat me? He said it was because I ate in a very unladylike way. I was embarrassing him, causing him to lose face with his friends."*

Rejection, violence and cruelty: not just for a few weeks but for decades. How to defend oneself under such an incessant onslaught? Void became hard and inflexible. She showed no compassion to her children, no love to her husband and no honour in herself. She felt she was not treasured by those she loved and so she chose to treasured no one. Motherhood was an obligation imposed on her by nature, not a choice she made. Marriage was simply an economic necessity. In Void's mind, a violent, loveless marriage was far better than no marriage. A cold, loveless home was safer than the street.

A Good Woman

In any life, dominant narratives emerge. We imagine ourselves through language and are duly created through the narratives that language engenders. The dominant narrative in Void's life framed around 'the good woman' – in itself, a simple term but when one unpicks the skin of it, the pulsating reality is revealed.

What makes a 'good woman' can never be fully answered because such a term, subjective as it is, remains in the eyes, mind and imagination of the beholder. For Void, however, there was no ambiguity in the concept of a 'good woman', it was as clear to her as the pain in her heart.

> *"A good woman? Yes, I have tried to be that, and a good wife and mother. It means I don't put myself first, I put my husband first because he is the provider. Without him the family cannot survive. I needed first my father, and then my husband, to protect me. It didn't matter if they didn't love me, care for me, or were kind to me, I just needed protection. A good woman is one who puts her duty as a woman before themselves."*

Duty and familial responsibility make a 'good woman'. At least for Void. She sees herself, after nearly eight decades of unhappiness, not as a victim but as a determined survivor. She bore and raised four children and has cared for grandchildren into her old age. What more can be expected of a woman and what more can a woman give? These are the questions and answers to which Void always retreated to when the endurable became unendurable.

Narratives don't come without a script attached, and the script that configures the 'good woman' is ages old. It invokes a loyal and faithful wife, the birth mother. Perhaps it was the first script ever written for the female of the species. Certainly, women of every race and ethnicity have been reading from this script all their lives and down through the generations.

Void never stopped reading the script. What is more, she believed it. Indeed, she became a zealous supporter of the script – the narrative and the unshakeable belief that men and women have clearly demarked and separate roles and that only through adhering to such roles can society, and families, be sustained especially through difficult times.

As the years unfolded Void passed on the good woman script to her two daughters and to her two daughters-in-law. They were a younger generation but one that Void had no doubt needed to follow the script and to create themselves around the narrative of woman as servant to the man, just as she had. In so doing, she sought to give justification to her own wretched condition.

The good woman narrative may appear logical to those who structure their existence around an inflexible gender binary, but it comes at a cost to the individual and to those who are subject to it – children and especially girls.

It is a conditioning term intended to reduce opportunity and, at its core, hope. There is no hope for a woman who believes her goodness relies on self-sacrifice, who willingly restricts herself to being a servant and who cannot imagine anything better for herself.

And with cruel logic, Void duly imagined nothing better for her daughters or her daughters-in-law. They were all required to follow the script and if they veered in any way at all, punishment ensued. The fierceness of Void's retribution for those who challenged the good woman narrative was particularly felt by her better educated daughter-in-law. She was never forgiven for seeking, as Void saw it, to diminish the authority of her son through her incessant pursuit of independent thinking and action.

By the time Void reached her sixties, she had forced the good woman script on every female member of her family. These women were required to obey their husbands; to never even imagine separation and certainly not divorce; to accede to their husbands' every demand; and work only to keep the family together.

Was there rebellion amongst these women? Yes. But mostly there was compliance, at least levels of it.

The term 'narrative' appears at first to be quite benign but it is not. It is immensely powerful because narrative informs identity and our identity is something we must protect at all times. Lose our identity and what have we left? It is the ultimate existential question. The good woman narrative, and the scripts that accompany it, cannot be easily rejected. They are not only rooted in history, they are rooted in culture. They surfaced in Void's family and in her husband's family. They were taught to her in primary school, they were reinforced in her village in everyday conversations with other women. To not believe in this narrative way of being was to not believe in her self, as a woman.

Payback

Many women who find themselves in the void of emptiness created by an unloving, harsh, abusive relationship, find solace in religion. In whatever scriptures, they can read words that may sustain them through long, lonely, cold days and nights. But religions require belief in the metaphysical, the unseen. They require devotion to a (male) deity who watches over them with understanding and empathy. Their message is invariably one of kindness, compassion and peace of mind. Void was not kind, she was not compassionate, and the only peace of mind she felt was when her children obeyed her and her husband was not at home. Void was a realist, not an idealist. She saw no point in following a belief system unless it put bread on the table and fuel on the fire.

Nevertheless, Void felt it wise to hedge her bets.

> "I would go to the temple with my children but only on special days. Why did I go? Well not because I believed everything I was told by the temple elders, but because I wanted the Gods to protect me, to bring me good fortune. When I had a little extra money I would always do the lottery. I never won any large amount but not doing the lottery meant I was guaranteed not to win anything. For me, praying to the Gods was no different."

The Gods never answered Void in terms of filling her purse, but as she saw it they did eventually provide a respite in her life. That respite was karma.

No young couples ever imagine a future where one of them is totally reliant on the benevolence of the other. And why should they? To be young is, for most, to be blessed with the bounties of health, strength and energy. But all that will fade over time and disappear. And when it does who will be there to save and protect you? Who will be there to nurse you, to minster to your daily needs? If you are lucky, and have good karma, there will be someone to do that who loves you and treasures you.

Void didn't love and treasure her husband. She feared and loathed him.

The young robust man grew old, infirm and weak. The husband who had hated and humiliated her, now relied upon her totally. The powerful patriarch lost his masculine energy and with it his male pride. There is not much pride left for a man when his wife needs to wipe his bottom because he is incapable of doing it for himself. There is not much pride left for a man when he can simply be ignored, shut in his bedroom for hours at a time and left alone.

This was payback time and Void didn't disappoint the karma placed before her. Her toxic femininity about-turned and with venom confronted one of its arch-creators. The good wife made sure her husband had enough to eat and a bed to sleep on, but that was all. He was isolated at home, denied access to his male friends and slapped around the face when he spoke to her in his old harsh manner. She would let him sleep in his own filth if the mood took her. His ears heard only harsh and cruel words, hatred and disdain. Her coldness towards him was icy – and vicious. On one occasion she pushed him to the floor so violently, his right arm was broken.

Fear of her husband had turned to mockery at his frailty and helplessness. Loathing multiplied. The final few years of the husband's life were filled with some of the humiliation, pain and suffering he had handed-out to his wife. In his twilight time he learned what it was like to be powerless and at the mercy of someone who finds you disgusting.

The Family

The human race needs myths because they serve an important purpose – they offer an ideal world, one far removed from reality. Their second purpose is to control. Myths provide social models to follow and standards and expectations of behaviour we are expected to adhere to. Of course, humans don't adhere to these expectations because life is far too messy to package in such simplistic ways. Nevertheless, the myths hang over us like an ever-present judgemental gaze, telling us 'this is how you should be, this is how your life should be.'

Arguably the most powerful global myth is that concerned with the family. The perfect family myth, where all members exist in harmony, love and mutual support, is one no person can ignore. And nor could Void and her family.

After her husband died, Void could have chosen to repair the damage he had caused her and the family. She could have sought solace in mindful reflection, forgiveness, kindness and hope. She could have strived if not for an ideal family, at least for an emotionally healthy one.

She did none of these things. Instead, she allowed the toxic femininity that had grown in her to fester and swell.

One of her sons turned to drink and was never able to overcome his alcoholism. The second son was tortured by shame and regret, taking this out on his own wife and family resulting in a divorce. The eldest daughter bravely attempted to follow her mother's instructions to always be a 'good wife', but herself succumbed to toxic femininity. The youngest daughter got away from the family home as soon as she was old enough to do so.

Any attempts at sweetness and love within the family were quickly destroyed by Void's poisonous aura. No matter how well her children and in-laws treated her, she remained coarse, harsh and critical of everyone. She had become incapable of receiving kindness, care, respect and empathy. She had become impossible to love. Good people – friends, family and neighbours – quickly left the orbit of Void's family, keeping their physical and emotional distance. It was safer and healthier for them if they stayed away.

Void's toxic femininity had the force and power of black hole at the heart of her family into which plunged any hope of forgiveness and joy; swallowing goodness as effectively as the black holes in space swallow light. Only suffering, abuse, pain and ugliness came out of this family black hole.

Void knew what the perfect family myth was, but in her case, reality won.

The Future?

Void's story has no happy ending. At the age of seventy-eight she suffered a stroke and while she is still able to communicate effectively, her ability to walk is limited. Her few female friends have either passed away or are also infirm and immobile. One son visits regularly, and a daughter remains close to her, though this daughter's story is also one of toxic femininity – a legacy from Void.

Void rarely had pleasure in her life, though she finds a little nowadays in her boisterous grandchildren. She has become the matriarch of a large and growing family. This gives her a power she never before had in her life. That makes her feel stronger and validated. To be sure, that power has not, and does not, go unchallenged, especially by one daughter-in-law. And it seems unlikely that Void will see her grand-daughters embrace traditional gender values in such a blind, devoted and uncritical manner. Void would likely consider that her greatest disappointment.

But the true sadness of Void's story concerns internalised rejection. From the age of six months the rejection she experienced took root in her unconsciousness, diminishing her esteem and in so doing, her capacity for agency. It sapped her will and any desire she might have had to be free of the abuse she suffered.

The armour that Void built around her over many decades proved a strong defence against loneliness and indifference. That armour was reinforced by the good woman narrative and her conviction that no woman can or should expect to stand alone. She must have a man to protect her, even if that man is a monster.

But if you accept submission what is left of you? Who are you if you are reduced to being the property of another? If you have no will to choose and shape your life, what sort of life have you?

These questions are unlikely to have ever entered Void's mind. And anyway, she was never one for critical reflection it was easier to just endure and get on with it. At least that way one got through the day, numbed the pain and soothed the loneliness. Work routine and the sheer weight of being a mother with four children, no money and a worthless husband, kept her mind occupied enough. Life was what it was. Just endure.

But the toxic femininity, that daughter of toxic masculinity, grew in Void. The armour that had protected her all those years became a straightjacket. She was trapped in it. She subsequently found hate and anger easier to express than compassion and empathy. Venomous words became a habit. Void was especially emotional cruel to those who aspired to a better life, especially the females in her family.

Hate is the meanest emotion but also the easiest to express. Hate and judgement come easy; love and acceptance are difficult. Resentment and envy flourish with shallow roots; generosity and empathy need careful nurturing in order to grow and flower.

Toxic femininity cannot nurture unconditional love. Most importantly, it cannot nurture self-love.

If you succumb to anger, hate and toxicity, what does that do to your soul, to your self-view?

Void never chose this life path. It was set out for her at birth. Circumstances conspired to create a miserable sentient being, trying hard to get through life and survive. She sought solace in the belief that as a woman, this was her lot. She never looked for ways out because such doors were not open to her, or so she thought. She deserves our sympathy and empathy for the trials and tribulations she was put through.

But she still made decisions.

Void had moments when she could have turned away from toxic femininity, especially after her husband passed away. But by then, life had probably hollowed Void out. It had emptied her of pity, kindness and reduced the possibility of forgiveness, not least her forgiveness for her own actions.

As Void's story reaches its conclusion there is no redemption only sufferance to the last moment. That final day in her life will at least in one respect be identical to every other day of her life. It will not be blessed with self-love.

Void will pass into the void never having loved herself. She will have only endured.

> *The night is swelling upwards, the day is elapsing into oblivion*
> *A lone bird is wallowing in the darkened frosty sky...*
> *Oh, unfathomed regret in me – for a life's pointless ferocity,*
> *For immense helplessness, and boundless deficiency!*

Chapter Six: Lost

Living But Not With Her Self

History can appear a foreign country, inhabited by a strange if not alien people living in strange if not alien times. But the truth is, we all get trapped by history. And a great many of us never escape it. Those that cannot escape live out the past every day of their lives, remorselessly and yet unknowingly. In this way humans are condemned to repeat history; all the mistakes and ensuing tragedies that occurred long before we were even conceived are predictably recreated for ours and future generations. We may imagine ourselves to be modern and contemporary and in our fashions and styles we probably are. But not in our heads. In our heads we are ancient, old and dated.

If we choose to be.

Lost chose to be.

As Void's eldest daughter, Lost didn't draw the winning numbers in life's lottery. She was losing from the start, born innocently and unwittingly into a vortex of violence and anger, where bitterness and recrimination overwhelmed kindness and compassion. Where cruel and harsh words dominated the family conversations, and where the safest place for Lost and her siblings was outside the home.

And then there was the poverty. The year that Lost was born, 1969, was one of great hardship for her community. The harvest had failed, hunger was growing into famine for most every family and life was, for many of Lost's generation, truly 'nasty, brutish and short'.

Despite her inauspicious start in life, fifty-one years later Lost has not only grown into a strong and determined woman, she has a successful career as a senior manager in the city's top hotel, two healthy children and a twenty-year-long marriage that began as a High School romance.

Poverty can be a grinder for some, a springboard for others. It all depends on that intangible mix of luck and effort. For Lost, poverty was a springboard. Even as a prepubescent girl she'd decided that hunger and cast-off clothing were not for her, which is why she waited nine years before marrying her childhood sweetheart. She put her career before her desires.

In that respect at least, she'd assimilated some of her mother's inner strength and resolution.

However, Void also left her daughter another 'gift', one not so positive – her femininity.

That is why today, Lost's bank account may full and healthy but her emotional account is not.

The Early Years

Every female has to contend with the 'gaze' – and with it the judgement on her actions and especially her body and appearance. This censorious gaze on the female is particularly potent when coming from other females. Is she one of us? Does she 'measure up' or not? Lost didn't measure up. She was blessed with intelligence but not beauty. Lost was born to be plain, ordinary and plump. She had not been gifted the beauty gene like many of her female friends. During puberty, her sexually formative years, she'd have happily swopped her intelligence for a little less plumpness and a better skin complexion. But intelligence does have its advantages in the competition for male attention. At High School she noted the most handsome boy, the nice, sociable youth her female friends contemplated, and won his heart. She did this through a simple strategy of understanding his fragile male ego. She recognised that behind the dishy features he was shy and insecure – and then ensured that everything she did for him, said to him, gave him confidence. Lost then spent much of the next thirty-five years continuing to do precisely that.

By the time she and her future husband left High School together, Lost was embarking on a career in hotel management, while he was embarking on no career at all, other than helping out at his family's Mom 'n' Pop shop. Her boyfriend was attractive but he was no match for Lost when it came to brain power.

During these early years, not only did Lost have to contend with a negative female gaze from her peers, she had to contend with at best indifference from her mother and father. Adversity and toxicity seemed to stalk the family like a ravenous wolf pack – there was no escape. But Lost did see an escape route – through hard work, discipline and education. She also adopted some of her boyfriend's social skills, recognising that if she were to climb out of poverty then she'd need some help.

Three years into technical college, help duly came along in the form of a friend's invitation to apply for a trainee management job with an international hotel group based in the capital city. This was a great opportunity. Few women from Lost's township got the chance to work in the city and certainly not in a well-paid, high status, secure job. Her decision to delay marriage and children had paid off. It would mean moving from her family home but she saw that as a bonus. Now she and her fiancé could plan their family life together.

When Lost began her hotel management career she was twenty-eight. She got married two years later. What had she learned up until that point?

Firstly, she'd learned to be patient. Nothing good comes quickly, so she reasoned. She'd also learned to be cautious and strategic; once she set her mind on a goal she aimed to achieve it. And perhaps most importantly, Lost had learned to be brave: she needed to be in order to survive the toxicity of her upbringing. She still loved her mother and father, but the violence and abuse she'd experienced and witnessed from childhood had left its mark on her soul.

> "I don't recall a time during my childhood when I felt completely safe. The family home was not a happy one. I tried to keep myself to myself and away from my father and mother. My two brothers got the worst of it, beatings and abuse. But we all suffered. But poverty meant I couldn't leave home after I graduated from High School. I wanted to continue to college but had no money so needed to stay at home. By then I was in love with my future husband so life was better even though we couldn't get married at that time."

What did Lost seek more than anything? She sought material comfort, a good income, security, a stable family life, healthy children, but perhaps most of all, respect. She wanted to be accepted, to belong, but to a better world than the one she'd been brought up in.

A career in management promised all of these and more besides. Lost could look forward to never having to worry about money again, never having to hold her head in shame because of her family's behaviour.

Lost likely didn't realise it when she was twenty-eight, but to achieve all this she would need to conform and obey. She would need to devise techniques to survive and thrive, especially in her marriage.

Therein lay the seeds of her own tragedy. For in being willing to compromise and accommodate, Lost would come to betray herself; elevating her husband but in the process devaluing herself.

Marriage

Nine years of courtship had not dulled the love which Lost and her husband felt for each other. The desire had never waned and nor had their mutual need. But those first years of marriage were not easy. Lost was embarking on a lifetime career in hospitality but what of her husband, what were his prospects?

He had no higher education but he had gym instructor skills, so he could possibly teach physical education. Fortunately, just as they were starting their married life, opportunities arose in the state education system for unqualified but skilled classroom assistants with exactly such skills. These part-time casual jobs didn't pay enough for him to quit his work in a local store, but they gave him an opportunity for extra income and higher respect in the community. Within two years he was employed on an annual contract as a classroom assistant at a primary school. He could at least claim a professional status on par with his wife's. What he couldn't claim was to be earning as much as her.

Once the children started arriving, so did the signs of toxicity in her husband. There were the occasional slaps, the cruel words, the accusations of infidelity, the anger, the jealousy. The four children were born in fairly rapid succession, but her husband never played any role in their upbringing, even though Lost was holding down a full-time management job requiring her to work shift hours, sometimes overnight in the hotel.

> *"My husband has two jobs so it is hard for him. When he finishes teaching he has a couple of hours spare before starting work in a local store. He needs an afternoon nap. But you know what young children are like. They can start crying anytime. Often the crying child would wake my husband up from his afternoon sleep and he'd be so angry he'd lash out and hit me."*

Lost was now learning another lesson – how to stay married to a man with toxic masculinity.

To the outside world her husband seemed a really good catch; sociable, fair, supportive and good looking. But this was not the complete picture. At home he was dominating, abusive and often violent.

Adapting to Toxic Masculinity

Just like Void, Lost chose to normalise her husband's toxic behaviour. She reasoned this was what all men were like and women were forced to put up with it, if they were to stay in a marriage or a relationship. After all, each of

Lost's men in her life – father, father-in-law, grandfathers, brothers and now her husband, had behaved like this. How could she expect her husband to be any different?

> *"You have to accept that men have a need to dominate, a desire to be seen as the head of the household. Women are the carers, men are the providers. This is how it's always been."*

This acquiescence to the traditional gender binary and the gender roles it enforces, seemed entirely natural to Lost and not too big a price to pay for peace and quiet at home. But it required her to conform, and even more than that, to appear subordinate. She had to become deferential and obedient to her husband, even, or especially, if that was not what she felt inside.

In other words, in order to keep her husband onside, Lost had to deny her own authentic identity. She had to betray her potential for independence.

An example of this betrayal is silence. Lost never challenged her husband's world view. She never risked an argument with him over any family or work matter. She allowed him to rule as 'man of the house'. His word was, and still is, law. In so doing, Lost denied herself an opinion.

But Lost also had a practical problem – within a few years she was earning more than her husband. In fact, by the age of forty-five, her salary was double his.

> *"I have never told him how much I earn. He would be too angry. Too jealous. It would make him feel inferior to me so not worth the risk. He thinks I earn half what I actually do. I give that half to him but the other half goes in my private bank account. He knows nothing about this money."*

For those of us who enter relationships assuming they will proceed on a basis of equality, mutuality, and shared trials and joys, Lost's approach to marriage will seem self-defeating if not complicit.

At the very least, it raises some questions.

How is it, for example, that a woman can actually make the effort to always appear small, low, poorer and less capable than her husband, when in truth it is the other way around?

How is it a woman can decide to suffer all the micro-aggressions of toxic masculinity in her husband and still hold on to the belief that this is entirely natural male behaviour?

How is it a woman will strive to appease her toxic husband, choosing always to bend her will and moreover that of her children, so as to keep him happy?

And if all that were not enough, Lost goes a step further in her journey of self-humiliation and identity denial – she changes her appearance.

In her mid-forties Lost noted a change in her husband's sexual behaviour – he became less interested in sex and indeed in any form of physical intimacy with her. Panicking and fearful that he might have a secret lover, Lost decided to change her appearance. This process began with a dramatic change in hairstyle. Gone was the long black straight hair to be replaced with short, blond curly hair. Gone were the simple print dresses to be replaced by designer jeans and body-hugging tops.

Her husband was furious and denounced her.

> *"He called me a slut, a whore, a cheap woman who was looking for other men. I was shocked and ashamed of myself. I just wanted to look more pretty for him but it made him reject me even more than before. So the next day I went and had my hair changed back to its normal black colour."*

Then something unexpected happened – her husband softened. Once he'd gotten over the shock of Lost's new appearance he encouraged her to change even more.

> *"When I was forty-seven I had a lot of plastic surgery done. Firstly, my eyes were made larger and then my lips were filled out. I changed my hair colour to red and kept it short and curly. It was what my husband wanted. I wanted to look younger for him, more desirable."*

Lost's response has been always to please her husband, put him first. Sure, there is the fear of how he might react if she angers him and the fear of losing him, but that is not what underpins this toxic family life. What underpins it are lies.

Firstly, the lie that all men are like her husband and that traditional gender roles are natural and normal.

Secondly, the lie that Lost as a wife is a complete, authentic woman who is being true to her self.

Two lies can never make a truth, which leaves Lost having to live with the lies, her invisible self, and yet somehow appear complete, contented and authentic to the outside world.

It is precisely under such impossible conditions and stresses that toxic femininity takes root.

Lost's Toxicity

Toxic femininity can be both internalised and externalised. In Lost's case, toxic femininity is internalised through diminishing her capacity for agency and is externalised as nastiness to other women. But to be expressed outwards it needs an arena, a target.

At the age of forty-eight, Lost was promoted to hotel manager. This gave her not just more income but also more power. And it gave her targets for her now fully-fledged, externalised, toxic femininity. In effect, she became a toxic leader, lashing out at junior employees and trainees, women especially. She had skills as a leader, including strategic planning and ensuring the hotel ran to the highest standards of security, cleanliness and customer care, but Lost was not an understanding leader – she expected to have her decisions followed without question and could be emotionally cruel to junior, pretty, women employees.

In effect, Lost lives two lives and thereby inhabits two identities; the pliant and passive wife and the fearsome, often cold-hearted Hotel Manager.

Is Lost aware of her dichotomous identity?

To be aware would require her to be reflective and that is not one of Lost's qualities. She is, however, strategic. For there is a third arena within which Lost operates and that is in relation to her bosses.

When it comes to her relationships with those who have power over her, notably the senior leaders in her hotel group she adopts an altogether softer, nicer and less dominating style. She will listen rather than talk and when she does talk it is with a smile and kind words. Lost cannot be unaware of the way she adapts to and differentiates between people and situations though it is unlikely she realises what is at the heart of these adaptions – her vulnerability as a woman.

Since childhood, Lost has striven for one goal – to not be vulnerable. Every major decision in her life, from choosing her husband to changing her looks, from striving for money to appeasing toxic masculinity, from delaying marriage to being obsequious with her bosses, has been based on her inner need for security.

But of course, no person is entirely secure. None of us know what tomorrow brings. We are all forever at risk of accident, trauma, illness and simply bad luck. We just have to learn to live with knowing there is an existential chasm over which we hover.

Unfortunately for Lost, her upbringing and belief in a natural 'gender order' only serve to make her even more vulnerable, more in need of love and acceptance, but sadly less able to realise a more agentic and positive femininity.

Challenges

When a woman unwittingly embraces toxic femininity, it can be a shock if confronted by women who do not support her world view. In Lost's case, there are two women in her life who very definitely challenge her.

Sister-in-Law: If there is one woman that Lost might admit to loathing, it is her sister-in-law, married to her younger brother. And the reason is that this woman is everything Lost is not: independent, feminist, challenging, highly educated and embracing an agentic and independent femininity. She is strong, rational, kind and reflective, all of which has, unsurprisingly, caused problems in the family. The sister-in-law has recently initiated divorce proceedings though this doesn't allow her to totally disconnect from the family. After all, there are the two grandchildren to consider and Lost is their aunty. The impending divorce has only served to make Lost (and her mother, Void) even more vocally critical of the "snake in the family" though one might ask to what extent Lost's anger is partly fuelled by envy at her sister-in-law's free will and sovereignty.

Daughter: Lost might put the sister-in-law problem down to her brother choosing the wrong wife but she cannot so easily do the same for her daughter's attitude. Now nearing seventeen, her daughter is demonstrating all the dominant gender attitudes of her generation. She is independent-minded, rejects traditional gender values and sexual mores, feels strongly about women having the right to choose whether or not to get married, have children, use contraception or have abortions. While it is not unusual for mothers and daughters to clash during the 'teenage years' all the signs point to an upcoming irrevocable split in the family on gender and generational lines, and especially between Lost and her daughter.

Where Is She Now?

Our fifth decade is one when we are most likely to undertake a life audit. We may not do this as an accountant might audit a company, but nevertheless we do undertake a review and evaluation, even subconsciously. After all, the sixties are looming and therein awaits massive life changes for most people. So best to start some planning and preparation, but most of all, some reflection on what our life's been like so far and how we might improve it.

If Lost were to undertake such an appraisal of her life so far, having reached the age of fifty-one, what would she conclude?

On the plus side she might well conclude that her life has been a lot more pleasant, successful, healthier, happier and less toxic than Void's, her troubled mother. She has more agency than her mother, a better life materially, and the prospects for her children look very good indeed. Lost has a career, something Void could not have even imagined for herself. Lost also has a husband and despite his behaviour, they've managed to stay together since High School. She also has the benefit of seeing her husband liked by others. He is sociable and generous and with his two jobs, one as a primary school teaching assistant, makes a major contribution to the household finances.

For a female born into acute poverty and deprivation, Lost has done impressively well. She has discovered how to be strategic at work and at home. She has discovered she can be brave and determined when others might give up. And she has developed the qualities of patience and fortitude.

Most importantly, she has managed to pass many of these qualities on to her daughter, though unwittingly also passing on to her a strong feminist consciousness. It therefore looks unlikely that her daughter will continue to cascade toxic femininity down through the future generations of females in her family. Hopefully, toxic femininity stops with Lost.

All this reveals a healthy account on the Credit side.

What about the Debit account?

Firstly, it is important to recognise that Lost is not supporting her daughter's desire for an independent life; Lost is pressuring her to conform to her way of thinking. If Lost had her way, her daughter will turn into yet another passive, pliant wife of yet another toxic male. Indeed, if her daughter did become such a woman, Lost would be overjoyed. Why? Because she'd see it as validation of her own world view, confirmation that her own approach to marriage and life itself was the best if not the only way. In short, if her daughter avoids repeating toxic femininity in her life it won't be because of her mother, it will be despite her mother.

What happens between Lost and her daughter could be the most important lesson Lost learns in life. If her daughter can stay strong and sufficiently independent minded to follow her own wishes, fulfilling her own agentic identity, then it cannot but have a profound effect on how Lost sees her own life. It could well cause some real soul-searching. Though not for a while yet.

Although it seems promising that Lost will not be able to pass on the toxic femininity virus to her daughter, it is too late for her. She succumbed a long, long time ago.

There is an image which forms in the mind when seeing Lost today. It is a stark and sad physical image underpinned by a depressing emotional reality.

The image is of a sex doll. Created by men, to serve men. It exists solely to please men. The sex doll has all the physical features that many men find attractive – the short curly red hair, the full body, the rich ruby lips, the wide, innocent eyes, and, crucially, it never answers back. Do what you like with it, say what you like to it, treat it any way you wish, the sex doll is always there for you. It is not asked for an opinion because it's not expected to have one. It is not asked if it is happy and contented, because the owner doesn't care either way. To be sure, the sex doll may be loved and cherished, but only so long as it pleases the owner, only so long as it continues to serve him. The day he gets bored with it, it is discarded, usually to be replaced by another one.

But Lost is not a doll. She is a real woman. A fully functioning, intelligent and brave person, someone who has strived to do the best for herself and her family all her life.

What is tragic, therefore, is how that brave and strong woman submitted to being a superficial needy person, with no self-respect, little self-validation, almost no self-expression, no personal development and hardly any self-love.

Like her mother, Lost is a survivor, but at a price. She has thrived materially but never truly lived. She is financially self-reliant but emotionally lost in the darkness.

She has the body of a sex doll and like the doll, lacks an authentic self. Lost is alive without ever having truly lived.

The ancient, old and dated thinking which configured Void, her mother, has been fully assimilated by Lost. In that way she is a victim of history, of a way of thinking and being a woman which places self-sacrifice and denial as a triumph, when in reality it is a disaster.

Lost is physically living in the twenty-first century but her mindset reflects a way of thinking that is fast disappearing over the horizon. And her daughter knows it.

To be sure, like all of us Lost has an authentic self, unfortunately she hasn't yet found it. And if she has she is not yet expressing it. It is likely to be deeply hidden in her and likely it will remain that way.

Having strived so hard to avoid being vulnerable, to be safe, Lost will safely make it to the graveyard, but without ever having discovered who she really could have been.

The night is near, you are here – another nowhere
Haven't those endless searches exhausted you, little heart?
Don't you hear the silent whisper from the twilight reddened sky:
"Where are you heading? Your home's everywhere!"

2: The Battling Women

Chapter Seven: Shame

WHERE LUST, LOVE AND TOXICITY COLLIDE

Life teaches us many lessons, though perhaps one of the most compelling for women especially, is learning how to separate lust from love. It is a lesson with many elements and many risks attached to failure. Add into the mix gender/sexual stereotypes, traditional cultures, toxic behaviours and insecure identities and the result can be disaster.

These disasters can ripple through lives like a tsunami.

This seems incredibly unfair, even cruel. For how many young people have the insight, wisdom, self-knowledge and experience to be able to distinguish between their quite natural sexual desires and their yearning for love and belonging? Not many. Probably none.

For sure, the road to adult maturity can be hard, rocky and precipitous, travelled alone and inevitably without a guide or map. Yet in our innocent youth none of this looks important. We are blessed with energy, optimism and aspirations, but also blinkers. We can never fully appreciate how decisions we take at, say, eighteen, might reverberate down the decades.

Actions have consequences. And as many of us discover, one act that can have the most profound consequences is the sex act.

This is rather tough given the inequity that societies invest in sex and sexuality. Wherever sexual libido emerges, there also arise two very different laws of unintended consequence – a liberal law for males and conservative law for females.

Or to put it another way, untrammelled sexual libido can offer an ego-boost for males, but shame and guilt for females.

Shame is not a biological condition – it is imposed on us by society, by our families and by our peers. Shame is a social control mechanism designed to ensure that humans behave according to prescribed rules and cultures. But which gender is most at risk of shame and shaming when it comes to sexual desire, lust and the sex act? Which gender is likely to carry the heaviest guilt load when it unwittingly slips between the lust and love gap? And which gender is most likely to be disgusted at its libido, not proud of it?

The journey of adulthood may well reveal the answers to these questions for each of us, though how we subsequently manage the lust-love dichotomy can never be predicted. Desire always has the potential to trip us up.

Just as it tripped up Shame.

Ashamed

It is a wintery January evening in a large city; blustery and cold. Few are venturing outdoors. But eighteen-year-old Shame and her mother have no choice. Mother is unwell, suffering from chronic back pain, which she wants to treat through natural medicine; traditional herbs. There is just such a clinic two blocks away. By the time they walk there, mother is weeping with pain, so she is relieved to find the young male clinician, to be welcoming, professional and sympathetic. He prescribes mother a cocktail of herbal medicines, recommending that they both stay in his clinic overnight to allow them to have full effect.

Within an hour, mother is asleep.

Ninety minutes later and Shame has given her virginity to the male clinician.

> *"Did I know this man? No. I had never met him before. Was it consensual? Yes. How did it happen? I don't know. I just remember him being kind, nice and understanding. He was handsome. My mother was asleep and not going to wake up until the morning. I'm not sure what I did to make him believe I wanted sex with him, must have been something. But one minute we were talking and laughing and the next he kissed me on the lips. I couldn't resist it, I didn't want to resist. A lot of my friends had already had sex with boys, classmates in our High School, but here was my chance to have sex with a man without anyone knowing. That was my first time. We slept together in the clinic, in the morning I took my mother home. No one in the family ever knew."*

The law of unintended consequences spared Shame a pregnancy but it gave her decades of guilt. Even now, aged forty-eight, she still vividly recalls that night not with joy at being desired and having the courage to express her sexual instincts, but shame at how she became as she puts it "sexually impure".

> *"I wanted sex. I didn't want to be a virgin any longer. I knew I was beautiful, desirable. Men looked at me all the time. I loved*

the attention, the fact that they wanted me. It gave me a feeling of power and made me feel like a woman. But I never forgave myself. I couldn't tell anyone about this. It was just too horrid, too disgusting. How had I given myself, my virginity, to a stranger? What sort of woman was I?!"

The second unintended consequence was the triggering of Shame's libido. She discovered her capacity to enjoy sex. She became a sexual being, but one riven with guilt. How to overcome this? She imagined the answer might lie with love.

Love

To be loved by someone who also sexually desires you, and to welcome that love is to experience a feeling of redemption. Aside from all the other emotions that come with love, personal validation is arguably one of the most significant. However we might feel about ourselves, we discover there exists in the world a person who loves us for who we are, and despite all our failings and weaknesses.

Just twelve months after her first sexual experience, Shame is immersed in such a love.

He is a fellow-student at the most prestigious university in the country. Like Shame, he is middle-class, intellectual and clever. He is also socially confident and ambitious. He is not burdened with guilt or shame over his libido. Just the opposite – sexual performance reinforces his masculine identity. Shame is not his first seduction; there have been several. Indeed, he is already in love with another student, besotted with her, before he meets Shame.

Shame then makes the second mistake in her life. She seduces this young man even while knowing he loves someone else. The opportunity arises when the man and his girlfriend fall out. Shame steps in. She loves the man, but this man, her husband-to-be, never stops loving the other woman. So begins her cycle of always being second.

"After the clinician, I never had sex with anyone until I met my future husband. He was already in a relationship but he chose to go with me. We started dating at university and began a sexual relationship almost immediately. After graduation, I went on to work in nursing and he went into architecture. We got married when we were twenty-five. Those first few years were perfect. We

were in love, we were enjoying our physical relationship, and our career prospects were excellent. I didn't need to think about sex with other men because I was satisfied and in love with my husband."

The first of two daughters was born two years later, by which time her marriage was fracturing.

"When did it start to go wrong? Oh, when my daughter was aged two, about five years into the marriage. I discovered he is having an affair with a work colleague. I was absolutely traumatized. Almost suicidal. I felt all the emotions – not just rejection, anger and jealously but also blame. I blamed myself. What had turned him away from me? What was wrong with me? But I still loved him, still desired him. I was about to begin an MBA and my own career was taking off. How to leave? I couldn't. I didn't want to be on my own as a single mother."

This marks the point in Shame's life when she begins to live a compartmentalised existence. On the surface she is an increasingly successful with a senior management post in a leading private hospital. She is ambitious and capable. She is a wife, mother and still blessed with beauty and a healthy body. Men continue to look at her with that interest that so excites her.

But the self-shame has not disappeared. Under the surface is a woman who feels rejected by the man she loves and whom she still desires, sexually. This feeling only serves to feed her self-loathing. She is disgusted with her actions and her sexual behaviour, so she disguises it as a need for love. Shame is needy, but where and how to satisfy these needs? Her zest for life remains but is marred by a growing feeling of inadequacy and frustration, all heightened by a moment of honesty and openness.

"I made a mistake telling my husband about my first sexual experience, with the clinician. I couldn't keep it a secret any longer. This happened after our daughter was born. I thought I could trust him with that knowledge. But I was badly mistaken. It was obvious what he thought. He thought I was promiscuous and was angry that I'd lied to him about being a virgin when he met me. He even said our daughter was not his, and accused me of sleeping around. I wasn't."

Warning Signs

Every journey starts with that first step. What was Shame's first step in her sexual awakening? It probably began in the clinician's arms. If so, then the second step took place at university, when she fell in love with the man she was to marry. But who was this man, really? How well did she know him? What was she committing herself to, in the name of love?

She was soon to find out.

> "My father-in-law was nasty towards his wife. Openly unfaithful, violent, and always looking to pick fights with her. The whole family is like this. My uncles-in-law and brother-in-law the same; negative, disloyal and disdainful to their wives. Never do any housework, dominating and dishonest. My husband is no different to them, though he can appear so kind and friendly to outsiders and at work."

Shame lost her sexual innocence at the age of eighteen. A decade later and she was losing whatever romantic innocence remained within her.

The toxic masculine family she had married into came to structure her world. Its values, behaviour and attitudes corrupted every member, reducing the womenfolk to mere possessions, sexual vassals of the men; women were there to exist only for men.

The warning signs were there from the outset. Shame could not miss the down-beaten mother-in-law, the brutal father-in-law, and the way in which male voices and opinions ruled.

But she was in love and she desired her husband, even to the extent of instrumentally wooing him away from his first love. And, of course, she continued to carry her own guilt-complex over her libido. Sex, to Shame, was not just a physical pleasure, it was a physical necessity. Love provided the route to sex, justified it and kept it 'legitimate' in Shame's mind.

Her love was sorely tested at times.

> "My husband likes to drink, and often came home from work, drunk. The first time he raped me he was drunk. I didn't want him, not at all, but he forced himself on me. Our daughter was only twelve months old and crying in the next room."

It is after one such episode of rape that Shame determines to take a different life path. She still pursues love and sex, but now outside of marriage.

Second-Best

The eighteen-year-old Shame stumbled into sex almost by accident, though not without agreement on her part. That young woman had a bright future and knew it. She was, rightly, filled with hope and anticipation. Sex, for her, was an energy deep inside that required satisfying, needed to be released. But within her society, the gender norm decreed she satisfy it through marriage.

She broke that norm once at eighteen and by the time she'd reached forty-eight, she'd broken it hundreds if not thousands of times more, with many different men.

The first was a security guard at a local hospital. She met him in a bar and began what was, for him at least, a love affair. It started out as a love affair for Shame too, though she accepted that love was going to be problematic given that he was married. So she settled for the sex. She was twenty-nine.

> "I was looking for love, a love to replace the one I'd felt for my husband. Instead I found sex but also a way of feeling good about myself, at least when those men first desired me. Some were work colleagues, others were just strangers I met in bars and then online."

She was looking for love, needing to be wanted for who she was as a woman, but being desired mostly for her body, and yet quite proud of that. But always second-best in the lives of these men, because almost Inevitably, they were married.

> "I kept experiencing the feeling of being in love, but it was fleeting. And all the while my life at home was miserable, lonely, and toxic. These men wanted my body but not me. Every sexual encounter ended in rejection. I was always the second woman in these men's lives. Never the first. In fact, I've never been the first woman in any man's life."

Unexpectedly, Shame got pregnant again, at the age of thirty-two, though she never told her husband and quietly had an abortion.

> "Was the child another man's? I don't think so. My husband and I still had an occasional physical relationship up until our early forties and I am sure the child was his. But I couldn't face having a second child at that time."

A second child did eventually arrive some years later – another daughter. And this daughter was to be a true blessing for Shame in her later years, though the child was to grow up in a highly toxic home.

> *"It got to the point where my husband, who was by now constantly unfaithful, would openly text other women while we sat together watching television. At least I was more discreet about my affairs."*

Two middle-class, successful professionals, husband and wife, two lovely healthy children, all living in a fine home in a posh suburb of a large city. He is admired and respected both socially and professionally. And so is she.

But behind the façade is distrust, lies, disloyalty – and shame.

Not that her husband feels shame: just the opposite. For him, every sexual conquest is just that, a conquest and therefore a validation of his masculinity and manliness. He openly boasts with his close male friends of the women he is seeing.

It is Shame who feels the self-loathing.

Living together but being apart: a familiar scenario in many a marriage. It wasn't meant to turn out that way. Neither Shame nor her husband fell in love expecting to fairly quickly fall out of it.

And yet, over a quarter of a century later, they are still together.

The Pattern

Relationships, and especially marriages, get built on habit. The routine of daily life and the rituals of being together, emotionally and physically, serve to reinforce the sense of security, togetherness and safety. Precisely because they are predictable, these patterns offer comfort to both parties.

The pattern that emerged in Shame's life was fairly well developed by the time she was forty and fifteen years into married life.

There would be a period of peace within the family home: no major arguments but no warmth or intimacy either. The focus would be on the children's welfare, schooling, and on their respective careers. Both Shame and her husband successfully maintained the public image of perfect family life to outsiders.

But within this routine there also existed dangerous triggers, where jealousy and anger could quickly flare up, blowing apart any pretence of familial normality.

For Shame, the triggers were her husband's continuing refusal to support her financially. He gave her a monthly amount for family needs but never anything more, despite his higher earnings. The second trigger was his drinking, typically he was coming home in the early hours drunk and abusive, and sometimes violent towards her. And the third trigger was his brazen attitude over his affairs. He made little effort to keep them secret.

Once a trigger was pulled, rows erupted, the family was in crisis, the atmosphere was poisonous and Shame descended into a very dark place.

Shame developed a set response to this situation – she went looking for love.

> *"There have always been men who desired me. I just followed up on it. I learned how to do so. This always happened when I felt really low. My work provides me with the opportunity to be away from the home so no one need know. Of course, my husband suspects but I don't tell him anything. We just continue with the marriage and the routine of married life."*

And so, over the years, the pattern developed: a period of peace, broken by a poisonous outpouring of anger and hatred, followed by Shame embarking on yet another search for love but also a search for sexual pleasure: Shame almost desperate to find someone who needs her so hopefully breaking the endless cycle of pain and rejection.

By the time Shame and her husband reached their mid-forties, any hope of marital reconciliation was lost. Both had been serially unfaithful. Both pursued sex with others for pleasure. Both sought love outside of the marriage.

But while Shame experienced rejection from the married men she dated, her husband found a second family.

> *"Yes, he has a second family now. And a son with the woman. He provides them with money and spends time there. He's never told me about them, I found out by accident when some documents addressed to this woman got wrongly sent to my home. He knows I know and that's enough."*

Shame's marriage was always a one-sided love affair. Shame certainly loved her husband but did he ever truly love her? Did he ever fully forgive her for trying to make him forget his first love at university? It seems unlikely because very soon into the marriage he began a new relationship, created a second family and even had another child with his lover. Shame successfully seduced her future husband but she never captured his heart. She married in hope of love from her husband but that love never arrived. But even before the marriage, Shame was already second-best.

Toxic Femininity

Many questions demand to be asked of Shame and her life so far but arguably the most compelling is; 'what happened to that bright, eager, vibrant, hopeful, fun-loving, young woman – where is she now?' Shame's life force stemmed in large part from her sexuality, her desires and her physical needs but that was also an expression of Shame's vitality and confidence. This is entirely natural, normal and healthy, but for Shame it turned toxic and has ended up almost devouring her. Look at her now and you see a hollowed-out woman. Her eyes cannot hide the sadness in her life.

Shame started out with more prospects and expectations than most other women, but has now arrived at a place of wretchedness and despair, and the reason for this is toxic femininity.

The toxic femininity within Shame is not turned outwards towards others; it is turned inwards to herself. It eats her up and corrodes her sense of self-worth as effectively as cancer eats a body. This toxic femininity is created and driven by shame and guilt, first triggered by her allowing herself to be seduced by a married man, the clinician, when she was just eighteen, but since magnified by her instrumental seduction of her future husband, plus all the other sexual encounters she has had. Shame grew up having internalised the social and conventional norm of how a woman should behave, sexually, but then broke that norm numerous times – and intentionally.

Shame's toxic femininity can never be ameliorated by having more casual sex nor looking for love in bars.

Shame has realised so much in her life but mostly material and career success. She has not realized self-confidence. She has not realised self-appreciation. And she has certainly not realised self-love. Whatever self-love she had at eighteen is gone at forty-eight.

In truth, every man in her life, from her husband to the most casual sexual encounter, has rejected her, turned her away and not put her first. She has, tragically, become used to being number two. All Shame's efforts at finding pure love have only resulted in her finding rejection.

But why has Shame accepted being second all her life? Why does she not break this cycle of despair and pain? This woman is not without qualities and abilities. In her career she is focused, determined, respected and successful. You look at Shame and you still see a beautiful woman, albeit ageing. She dresses well, is smart and alluring. But then you look in her eyes and you see a deadness.

Hope?

What hope is there now for Shame?

There is hope in her children, at least one of them.

The eldest daughter, aged twenty-one, treats her mother with open disdain. This is a fractured, divided family, and her eldest daughter has sided with her father, effectively rejecting her mother.

But not her youngest daughter, now aged seventeen. This daughter demonstrates a lot of emotional intelligence and has developed a healthy and positive friendship with her mother. This is one of the few sources of comfort in Shame's family life.

On the minus side, Shame remains married and thus was wed into a cruel, misogynistic family of toxic males and submissive, beaten, women. Shame has taken her place amongst them – almost.

One can interpret Shame's decided and unremitting pursuit of sex and love outside of marriage as a form of resistance to toxic masculinity. It is an expression of her agency. Sex outside marriage is her choice. No one forces it upon her. She can and does use this to acquire some degree of self-actualisation but also to attack her husband, reminding him that she finds sexual pleasure with other men and reminding him of his own inadequacy as her husband. At least he no longer rapes her. They continue to live in a divided home, though in truth, it is not a home it is merely a place where four people reside, all related.

The real hope for Shame rests on her making two crucial decisions.

The first is to realise that the shame she has enveloped around herself and within her very being, is nothing more than a delusion. She has no reason to feel shame, certainly not because of the way she lost her virginity. Shame, at eighteen, was caught in the culture trap, the gendered values that prevailed in her society thirty years ago. Those gendered values are, thankfully, disappearing fast around the world.

Should she feel shame for the way she seduced her future husband? Certainly, she can feel some guilt because she acted in love but with strategic intent. She knew her future husband loved another woman but when an opportunity arose to seduce him she took it and without hesitation. Maybe her husband never forgave her for that, though he must take responsibility also.

There are very few innocents in Shame's story.

The second decision Shame must make is to no longer accept being second. So long as this demeaning condition continues, Shame cannot move on. She must find the self-respect to say no to unsuitable men, those who desire her body but not her-self.

Sex has been Shame's Achilles heel. She enjoys it. She finds it satisfying and physically rewarding. In those moments of sexual orgasm and seduction she is at peace with herself. But they are momentary. They cannot last longer than a few moments, maybe a few hours. After the sex, she must always return home. The orgasmic pleasure passes to be replaced by a sour and corrosive self-loathing.

To be sure, the men in her life desire her, but only ever for sex. These men want Shame to be in their life, but only as number two, never number one. She is their sex-buddy. Nothing more. And she knows all this.

However, it is not enough to be fully aware of being the loser in this complex, toxic, manipulative game of 'love'. One must know how to get out of it – how to change the game.

Weeping, Shame spoke these words:

> "I know what I must do. I must decide to no longer accept being second best for any man. I now recognize the pattern of choosing to be second. I am second because I have chosen to be. I must choose not to be. I must set higher my standards, both in myself and in men."

She must find a man who touches her soul, and avoid those who are only concerned with her body.

She must stop punishing herself for her desire for sex, her shame over how she has acted with men for over thirty years.

She must finally reconcile herself with who she is as a woman. She must stop seeing sex as inherently shameful. She must reject shame and guilt.

And she must stop expecting to find love only in the bedroom.

Two Very Different Possibilities for Shame:

Possibility 1: Her life will continue to be dark and cold. She will experience failure, pain and a creeping inner death. As she ages so will she become lonelier, more isolated and bitter. Sex will no longer be readily available to her as the decades role by and this will fill her with regret and frustration. Self-love will be a distant possibility.

> The flower, once scarlet, is nowhere to be seen
> The leaves, once voluptuous, now the colour of dirt
> The cloud, once charming, is no more in the sky
> The heart, once vibrant, is now a vain hollow.

Possibility 2: She will start to love herself and thereby begin the process of inner healing. She will accept where she has acted badly towards others and towards her-self, but not accept the sexual values which society has tried to impose on her since childhood. She will forgive herself and those around her, including her husband. But she will find real comfort from within and through a resurgent self-awareness. True love will then find her.

The prince on the ship
With scarlet sails will come,
When, and only when,
Your heart is a scarlet sail itself

Chapter Eight: Courage

In and Out of the Darkness

What is courage? How do we define it? How can we recognise it? What does it mean to be courageous? These are not simply philosophical questions, they are deeply personal ones. Very few humans go through life without being tested in some ways, very likely many ways. And the longer one lives the more tests there will be, some of which we may not pass.

In the final reckoning, perhaps courage is all we need, the most important asset of all to get us through life. But until we are tested none of us can truly know just how deep our resolve goes, just how strong we are. For we cannot claim to be courageous until the test is over, until we have endured and hopefully overcome whatever it was that life dumped on our lap and told us to 'get on with it.'

Across all human cultures, there arise similarly conventional notions of courage inevitably built around physical bravery, fearlessness in the face of great danger, valour and heroism in battle, boldness and daring.

But like much in human society, such notions are at best partial and at worse, completely misleading. They are narratives we humans create for ourselves; to explain the inexplicable, to provide models to emulate, to create icons to worship, to allow us to believe in super-heroes.

But what if we don't win? What if we try but fail? What if we can never fully overcome but instead have to endure? What if we are merely surviving? Does that mean we lack courage?

Do life's 'losers' lack courage?

On the face of it, and as many people might see her, not least her family, Courage is a loser. She is small, frail, demure, shy, and middle-aged. Even in the society to which she most earnestly desires to belong, she is, today, just another poor, struggling, single parent – invisible and unimportant.

And you too might well pass Courage in the street and not pay her a second glance.

But as you read her story perhaps something else will emerge in your understanding of Courage – respect, combined with optimism that this woman can overcome, deserves to overcome, and is worthy of a better life.

Belonging

Look into the eyes of a baby and you will see through to the core of what it means to be alive – the need to belong. Belonging is the essence of living – not only for humans but for all advanced species on earth. And where does that baby search for belonging? In its family – most likely with the adults that brought it into the world. The eyes of a baby implore you to love it, to want to hold it, to care for it. Of course, the baby has no concept of any of this. It is simply doing what human babies have done down the millennia – sought to survive using one of the few tools at its disposal; its irresistibility.

Courage was such a baby, and forty-five years ago her eyes similarly implored her parents to love her, to care for her, to protect her.

Unfortunately for Courage, her parents never did. They tolerated her and accepted her only as the unfavoured child.

Courage's parents already had a favoured child – her brother.

The circumstances of our life situation play a powerful role in how we come to express ourselves, and the circumstances of Courage's family were not auspicious. They were a low-income family living in a small town some 60 km from their country's capital city. With few if any prospects of bettering themselves, Courage's mother and father considered her brother to be of more value; their expectations being that as an adult he would support them during their retirement years. By contrast, Courage would get married and raise her own family. In effect, Courage would have to create her own family if she wanted to belong.

Does this gendered expectation excuse the fact that Courage received almost no material and emotional support from her parents? Who is to judge? But that is the reality.

The consequence of Courage being an outsider in her own family, of not receiving the protection and love she desired and needed as a child was an acute inferiority complex. She found it hard to believe she could achieve anything more than the limited expectations placed on her by her parents. She internalised the pathetic state offered to her as her only due.

Fortunately, Courage did have one asset in her favour – a good brain, which was helped develop by a reasonably efficient education system. At the age of eighteen she was offered a place at the city university, whereupon she left home to live with her more prosperous, city-dwelling aunt.

So began a seven-year period in Courage's life that was to see her acquire a BA in Accounting, quickly followed by an MA in Accounting. While the inferiority complex did not disappear, and Courage continued to struggle financially, socially and psychologically, at least she could now claim educational achievement.

At the age of twenty-five, Courage began working as a junior accountant in a large printing firm in the city. She was then as she is now, quiet, modest, and without any ambition whatsoever. If she had one hope it was to be average, to survive, to get by, but most of all to be accepted and to belong.

Not having an emotional anchor in her own family, she did as her parents expected – she got married. At least this offered her a new family to which she might belong. She hoped.

The Husband

Lacking any self-love and burdened by a deeply rooted inferiority complex about her abilities and appearance, Courage made the classic mistake that countless numbers of young women down the ages have made – she married the first man who showed any interest in her.

Not only was Courage a physical virgin, she was also an emotional one, so when a fellow-office worker paid her some compliments and then asked for a date, she was only too happy to agree.

> *"He was the first man I ever dated and the first and only man with whom I have had a physical relationship. I had no idea about relationships and even less about marriage. We got married six months later, when I was twenty-seven and he was thirty. Marriage seemed the natural next step in my life. It gave me a chance to start a family and have my own home in the city."*

The man Courage had chosen to marry and stake her future happiness on was less educated than her, had few career prospects, had only ever lived with his parents, and was lazy and indecisive. He also had expectations of being the boss in the home, with Courage as his subordinated wife.

There is no mention of love in Courage's account of her married life, and if that emotion was ever present it quickly disappeared when confronted by her husband's greatest weakness.

> *"I didn't know it before I married him but my husband was a gambler. He was a gambling addict."*

There are many reasons to avoid marrying a man, several red flags to look out for, at least if you hope for a stable and loving relationship. Unfortunately, Courage overlooked a good many of them. The marriage that she had hoped would bring security, comfort and belonging into her life, drove all of these out. The result was loneliness, coldness and an even greater sense of hopeless and inferiority.

At the age of thirty, Courage gave birth to the single joy in her life – a baby boy. He was to become not just a son but a close friend, though there were many challenges to overcome before those days arrived.

The first challenge was her husband's verbal violence towards her and the debt that his unremitting gambling forced on the family. In typical style, knowing only one way of dealing with such difficulties, Courage simply accepted the violence as her feminine lot and the debt as motivation to work longer and harder. This effort resulted in her getting promoted and eventually able to gain a higher-level accountancy job in a fast-developing IT firm. Her husband remained the lowly officer worker in the printing company that had previously employed Courage.

Courage was married but in truth she was now in survival mode. This marriage was no longer about expectations or even distant hopes of love and passion, but simply about surviving the daily trials and tests of her courage and ability to endure.

The Family

Courage didn't realise it when she was younger, more innocent and less aware, but the script to which her life was being played out had not been written for her benefit. The role she was expected to play demanded she conform and submit. As a woman, submission to her husband was her primary obligation – at least in the eyes of her family and her in-laws.

> *"I would return to my parents' home in tears, having suffered yet more abuse from my husband. We had no money – he gambled it away, and I had no love or comfort in my life. But my mother just turned around and said I had to obey my husband and that being a good wife meant being obedient and passive. This was the life my mother had had, and she expected me to be the same. I expected it be the same. I knew no other way. But it was terribly hard."*

Having been told very clearly by her own mother that she must continue in the marriage and that neither divorce nor separation were options, Courage found even less solace with her in-laws – they verbally attacked her, demeaned her, and rejected her. To them, she was little more than a slave. As with her own family, her husband's family treated wives as second-class citizens. They were there to serve, not be served. Whatever familial loyalty existed, none of it was reserved for Courage. As her husband saw it, family came first, not his wife.

> *"My husband made it very clear on many occasions that a wife can always be replaced but parents are irreplaceable."*

The extent of her husband's cruel indifference to his wife was made evident on those occasions when she was subjected to physical violence – not from her husband but from her father-in-law and even on at least one occasion, her husband's gambling friends. The depth to which Courage had sunk in her marriage and in her status as a woman, was made every evident one evening.

> *"It was one of the few times I lost my temper with my husband. We were having dinner and he told me to find him some more money. I knew why – he'd lost all his gambling in the poker den with his friends. Just at that time, one of his gambling friends phoned the house. I answered and told him to not bother us, that my husband was not going gambling tonight and to leave us alone."*

That male friend of her husband did not leave her alone. Instead, he immediately got in his car and drove to their home, whereupon he stormed up the stairs to their apartment, walked in and slapped Courage around the face and head. She crumbled to the floor, bruised and weeping.

> *"My husband did nothing. He just sat there at the dinner table. Then he got up and walked out with his friend. I didn't see him until the following evening when he came home for his dinner."*

Traditional masculinity and its values lie at the heart of Courage's story – they provide the toxicity that comes to poison every aspect of her life and in turn creates the toxic femininity which Courage internalises as helplessness, inferiority and passivity in the face of male aggression and cruelty.

But even traditional masculinity contains one redeeming feature – it is supposed to be protective of women, especially of wives and partners when they are exposed to aggression from other males.

Not so with Courage's husband. When he might have finally stood up and acted as a decent man, a decent husband, at the moment when he could have found some remnants of male dignity, he betrayed his wife. He rejected her and sided with his gambling pal. He simply looked on as Courage was beaten, then walked away, saying nothing.

If all this male aggression was intended as a lesson for Courage, presumably it was to remind her that she was less than nothing.

Humiliation, abuse, violence and ice cold indifference from those whom you should reasonably expect to love you and care for you. Plus, a feckless, lazy, gambling-addicted husband. What would be your breaking point? Where would your tolerance end?

Courage eventually found her breaking point and it arrived most unexpectedly.

Breaking Point

It was a warm spring Saturday morning and Courage was at home with her son. Her husband was in bed, sleeping off his previous night's gambling and drinking. Courage walked to the balcony of the second-floor apartment and looked out across the city. She heard familiar voices in the street below.

> *"Two women were talking, I could hear them quite clearly though they didn't know I was on my balcony and could hear them. One of them, a woman who owned an apartment next to mine, was talking about me to her friend. I couldn't believe what she said, it really upset me. She said I was lazy, a late sleeper and disobedient to my husband. They were gossiping about me and being quite nasty. After all my efforts to keep my family together, to suffer my husband's behaviour and put up with the endless criticism from my family and his, I just thought to myself, that's it. I am getting out of here."*

Courage was now aged forty. She had a decent job and was respected at work, but not respected where it really mattered – in her family. She was not even respected by other women, who themselves were suffering in abusive marriages. She had never felt more alone but neither had she felt more determined.

After years of silent submission, negative judgements from her parents, barbed comments from her in laws, and physical violence, Courage had finally reached her breaking point. She understood very clearly that there was no point continuing with the marriage. If she was to save herself she had to leave, and soon. But she also knew that her husband would not divorce her. If she was to move on then she had to physically move out.

Over the next few months, Courage planned her escape. She told no one about her intention to leave her husband. She had no one in her life whom she could trust, certainly not her parents.

But she did have a decent job and that gave her an excuse; it gave her cover.

Courage started to stay later at work, or so she told her husband. In truth, she would leave work at her normal time but then go and look for apartments in other parts of the city. She also did overtime at work during weekends and this extra money she put aside for her eventual departure.

Four months later, Courage was ready to leave. She had found a small apartment.

She moved on a weekday – taking a day's due holiday from work. The hired van came to the apartment after her husband had gone to work and all her belongings were piled into it and taken to the new apartment. Emptied of her personal items, the apartment was left for her husband to return to in the evening.

Her son, now aged ten, had no idea this was going to happen, not until she picked him up after school and took him to his new home.

> *"I had to do this secretly. I couldn't tell anyone. I was frightened what would happen if my husband found out I was intending to leave him. For six months I never told anyone where I was living. I put my son in a new school. I cut off all contact with my husband, his family, my family. Eventually, they all accepted I was not going to return to him. But then I had to get on with my life and it was not going to be easy."*

When we are pushed to breaking point, when we realise there is no point or possibility of continuing as we are doing, then that moment signals change in our lives. And yes, it takes courage to move on. But the real tests come later; the true courage is needed after the initial emotional eruption and when the cold-clarity of what we have started reveals itself.

The courage to get up every morning and continue.

The cold-clarity for Courage was physical and emotional isolation. The apartment was basic but just affordable. She had work colleagues but no close friends whom she could share her thoughts, fears and hopes with. Money was always tight. She could barely afford her son's school necessities, and there were no luxuries.

> *"Every day is a struggle, every day is a battlefield, I just try to stay unconquered. Much of the time I am afraid. I am afraid of never having anyone in my life who can love me as a woman. I am afraid of what my family think of me. But I am also afraid of giving up."*

True courage is revealed in the little things: the determination to ensure that the daily routine continues, that bills get paid, that children are protected and nurtured, and that there is food on the table every day. None of these simple tasks are inevitable. They have to be worked at. By leaving her husband and living as a single parent, Courage has lost the most precious thing in her life – her family. But then, did she ever really have one?

The Toxic Institution

A modest woman, of modest means – someone who would hurt no one and who only wants to be accepted and loved. How is it such a woman can end up enveloped in rejection, neglect, pain and cruelty? There is no single answer to such a question though there can be little doubt that family plays a major role in Courage having to live out such a cold and isolated existence.

The family that Courage was born into and the family in which she eventually found herself as a wife, were both fundamentally toxic. The toxicity arose from traditional gender values themselves reinforced and validated by traditional, toxic, masculinity. All the women connected with Courage's birth family suffered from this. In turn, they internalised that toxicity into their expression of femininity.

Courage's mother is unhappy, discontented, scoured by poverty and heavy domestic duties. She suffers from chronic stomach problems and failing health. Her toxic femininity realises itself in her physical body and in her emotional behaviour.

Thus arises, as a tragic inevitability, the toxic institution of the family, whereby toxic femininity become institutionalised down the ages, waiting to infect each new generation of females. From Courage's story, we know her mother had this condition and there is compelling evidence that Courage's mother picked it up from her own mother.

Alas for Courage, the family she married into also carried this virus, expressed as male dominance and the demand for female acquiescence. Men gave the orders, women obeyed. No one offered resistance; there was only acceptance that this was the 'natural' order of things. As Courage came to realise, she was little more than a servant to her husband and his family – she was never expected to be anything else. This was her future from the moment she was born and it was merely reinforced in her marriage, though the real pain arose from her mother's explicit support for her husband, not for her. That was the most cruel and heartless rejection for Courage.

One is entitled to ask, therefore, what is the point of the family as an institution, as a foundational brick of society, if its primary mission is to perpetuate a gender order that results in a form of servitude for women? What value a mother and father if they are complicit in the emotional traumatisation of their child?

Never has anyone stood up for Courage. Never has she had the comfort of knowing that her parents, especially her mother, would understand her agony and help her alleviate it. Never had she anyone to share the pain with, to even discuss her dilemma with. She was alone.

But was Courage's existence only ever one of receiving bitter words from her family and husband? No, Courage would be praised when she 'behaved well', when she complied with her parents' and in-laws' expectations, when she obeyed her husband and tolerated his feckless gambling and uselessness. Such praise, coming as it inevitably did in a desert of emotional emptiness, could be highly powerful and persuasive.

> *"There were times when I felt good about myself, and these came when I fitted in, did as was expected of me, never complained, never asked for more from my husband, but simply tolerated it all. Then he would praise me, tell me he loved me and valued me."*

Drunk on the cheap praise bestowed on her by a noxious husband, Courage fell into the trap that lies in wait within toxic femininity – the trap of low, if not absent, expectations. She took the praise as a thirsty person takes a drink – with relish if not gratitude. Little did she realise that she was, in effect, betraying herself. These weasel words of praise and love came easy from her husband; they meant nothing to him and were simply a means to ensure his wife's compliance to his authority. But every word spoken in praise and earnestly accepted by Courage, only reduced her further.

Ironically, it was words that triggered Courage's resistance – the words spoken by her neighbours and that she inadvertently overheard. In that moment she saw the truth of it all. She was not respected for trying to fit in. She was not considered a worthy wife, mother, daughter or woman. Despite her efforts to comply, she was nothing.

Decades of yielding and submission, of trying to be the woman, the daughter, the wife, the mother which society and her family demanded, resulted in her being denied the one thing she had most yearned for all her life – to belong.

It also denied her the possibility of self-love. For to find that self-love she first had to find her self-respect.

Where Is She Now?

> *"What is my greatest regret? Ever listening and believing in the stupid words of those women, including my mother, who told me I had to obey my husband."*

70

Self-awareness can be a slow if not painful process. It requires we let go of certain mistaken ideas, myths, and illusions that are holding us back from self-actualisation. The first illusion that Courage had to let go of, in order to find her self-respect, in order to start the journey to self-love, was the illusion that her mother was always right. The second illusion was the idea that only through marriage could she become a complete woman, worthwhile and valued. She had to stop obeying and start thinking for herself.

Courage has had to break free from a conventional family structure, which meant visibly living outside it – as a single mother. She has had to break free from social norms about a woman's role and requirement to be both a family breadwinner and full-time domestic worker and mother – she is all these things today, but on her terms, not those of her separated husband.

Today, Courage is on her own, physically, though her relationship with her fifteen-year-old son is especially strong. She is aware of what she must avoid in her son – any notion that being a male puts him above females.

But Courage is not so alone as she was when she was living with her husband. She discovered a way of validating herself against peer-pressure to conform and that was via social media.

The Blessing of Facebook

> *"Social media saved me in a way. I found online communities of similarly-minded women to which I could belong. One community is led by a Buddhist monk and another is led by a woman who teaches meditation and mindfulness. These act like virtual temples on Facebook and have helped me a lot. I feel treasured, loved and empowered through these communities. They have given me the strength to raise myself, improve, and transform.*
>
> *Am I still struggling? Yes. Some days are incredibly hard. I get tired and sad, depressed with my situation. There are many times when the old values and habits creep back into my mind. I think to myself, am I being a good mother, daughter? I still love my mother and feel compassion for her she is troubled also – but I have to protect myself."*

Social media gets a lot of criticism, especially regarding its negative impact on people's mental health and wellbeing. And to be sure, there are oceans of toxicity on Facebook and the rest. But as Courage puts it, you get back what you put in:

"I can only speak for myself and I know that without these virtual communities to support me through the darkest times, I doubt I could have survived. I would probably have returned to my husband and that would be my hope for a better life, gone. It seems to me that social media is like karma – you get back what you put in. I get back love, support, empathy and understanding. But that is what I put in too."

In and Out of the Darkness

This story of Courage is far from over, indeed the key element – her finding self-love – has only just begun. But she has taken the most important first step to independent living and independent femininity and that is to physically dissociate from her husband, his family, and to some extent, her own family.

Risks remain, not least her husband who is now trying his hardest to entice her back, using Courage's parents to pressure her to return him. He has started giving Courage money every month and he is making it difficult for Courage to proceed with the divorce – claiming certain documents have been lost that prove her residency status.

Where does that leave her? It leaves her still not fitting in to any community and it leaves her torn between what she needs for herself and what others demand from her. She is but a step along on the journey of self-reinvention and any number of unexpected situations could send her plunging down into the chasm. She may give up, surrender. Courage is today, physically, financially and emotionally, existing on the edge of oblivion. Her life is lived moving incessantly in and out of the darkness.

The nearest she can get to being part of a community, finding the belonging she desires, is via social media, and the mindfulness, wellbeing communities on Facebook. These are proving to be an unexpected and most welcome blessing for Courage – they give her unconditional love and emotional support. But they cannot replace the intimacy, love and belonging of a fully-fledged, happily-functioning, family. They cannot erase the years of pain and rejection, though in time they may well dampened that memory.

Courage is, at heart, a good, kind, soft, gentle, but still highly vulnerable woman. Courage is the name we have given her. It is not the name she would choose for herself.

But then, Courage wouldn't recognise her own self-worth. She is still striving for it. She is still striving to build her self-confidence, self-appreciation and self-love.

Inside Courage a battle rages, between the pull of the toxic past, and the push of a self-loving future. The result is emotional upheaval, sometimes chaos. Every day is a battle to not feel inferior, to feel worthy.

Her parents 'gifted' her the inferiority complex and her husband used it against her. She, and only she, can now reject that internalised toxic feminine identity and become the woman she is deserves to be; happy, self-reliant, and completely aware of her own value as a woman, no longer inferior to anyone.

The Hope

Courage's story may seem atypical in parts but many women are in exactly her situation. That is, they are in the process of developing self-validation, of moving from depending on the external validation provided by others (often a male partner) to relying on themselves, being sustained primarily by self-love; not needing anyone else's validation or love in order to feel complete and truly confident.

Our hope, therefore, is that the day will come when Courage is this self-sufficient, when she can validate herself well enough and when she needs no one else to say she belongs but rather she knows she belongs within her own being. When that day comes she'll not even need the mindful communities of Facebook.

Her heart is not yet strong enough, but hopefully one day it will be. She is striving for that.

This is what it means to be courageous. This is what is means to have courage – to keep pushing forwards even when the odds against you seem, at times, overwhelming.

Knowing Courage as we do, we believe she will make it and will find the better life she is so worthy of. Someone this brave, this resolute, must – despite the hurdles yet to overcome – achieve her ultimate goal which is to be at peace with herself, within herself; to live a life which is secure, easy, warm and carefree.

Please join us in wishing Courage every success in her life journey. Send her your positive energy – she deserves it.

And then, one day,
The tiny leaf finds the whole forest within its inner depth.

Chapter Nine: Princess

Is it possible to manifest ourselves into existence? That is, to have an image of ourselves in our head, which, consciously or not, we then actualise, bring into reality? Many psychologists and professional experts believe so. An example is the athlete who imagines herself stepping up to the podium to receive an Olympic gold medal. Top sports coaches will tell their athletes that unless they can imagine this scenario, with themselves as a winner, then there is not much chance of it actually happening.

Princess has never imagined herself as an Olympic winner, but she has always imagined herself as special, and expected to be treated as such. She has lived her life in pursuit of the dream of excellence and exclusivity; a woman apart, elevated if not idolized, especially by men.

And the first man to tell her she was a princess, was her father.

Upbringing

Princess was born and raised in what many might consider to be privileged circumstances. Her family were comfortably middle-class, highly educated professionals; her mother a school teacher; her father, a veterinary surgeon. The family lived in a beautiful home in a prosperous suburb of a rapidly developing city.

The eldest of three children, Princess relished being indulged by her parents. Until her brother was born when she was aged six, Princess was, indeed, treated as such by her parents. Thereafter, even while she was inevitably competing with her younger siblings for parental attention, Princess never doubted her entitlement. In her own mind, if not that of her parents, she was always number one.

This fervent self-belief in her own qualities, served Princess well as she was growing up. She observed and copied the behaviours of those women who were, indeed, special; the real-life princesses, the rich and famous women, and the powerful ones. By the time she'd reached her country's top university, to study literature, Princess could turn on her charm and her seductiveness like a light-switch. She was a man-magnet. Men were mesmerised by her. Blessed with a sharp wit, high intelligence, and charismatic style, Princess could captivate anyone. But this woman was not all pride and ego, because she was also honest, kind-hearted and generous.

Everything about the young Princess was larger than life – her talents, her abilities, her potential, and her expectations of what life was going to be like.

The monied life-style of her family not only provided a firm foundation upon which to build her life, it established high standards for Princess to follow and ideally to surpass. This, together with her father's boundless, uncritical devotion provided the basis upon which Princess internalised her self-worth, her self-love.

However, the self-love that Princess developed from an early age was not in balance. As her story reveals, Princess's self-love exists but is weak in a number of dimensions. And this imbalance is what has caused the manifestation of something much less appealing in Princess's character – toxic femininity.

Self-Appreciation

As we explained in the first chapter, self-love is not mono-dimensional, it is multi-dimensional.

And the dimension which Princess has most strongly is self-appreciation.

Princess values herself most highly.

She is not going to wait for a man to come along and place her on a pedestal. Princess has already placed herself on that pedestal. What she wants, what she needs, what she expects, is a man to place himself at the foot of that pedestal and, like her father, dote upon her.

In that regard, Princess is quite different to many of the women detailed in this book. For this is not a woman in search of someone to appreciate her and love her, thereby allowing her to appreciate and love herself.

Princess has buckets of self-appreciation, and a good dollop of self-love.

Princess is no Sleeping Beauty. She doesn't need a Prince to come along and give her the kiss of life and rescue her. What she needs from a man, indeed demands, is that he treats her like she's always expected to be treated – as royalty.

Princess believes she was born to be the best and it therefore follows that anyone who comes into her life or deems to enter her intimate orbit, should recognise that also.

Many women reading this will likely think to themselves; 'well, why not? Why shouldn't any woman expect this type of treatment? If a man claims to love his female partner, shouldn't he then treat her like royalty, like a Princess?'

Not if it results in the man getting sore knees from always being in a position of paying homage, and the woman getting vertigo from always having her head in the clouds.

As with life, relationships are all about balance, which can only be enabled through self-awareness, self-sufficiency, and inner-resilience.

Toxic femininity feeds off imbalance. And imbalance, both in her type of self-love and in her expectations of how loved ones and work colleagues should treat her, went on to create a multitude of problems for Princess. Decades on from when her father first called her 'my princess', such problems reduced her from royalty to pauper.

Following Her Heart

Princess has a big heart, and when it speaks, she listens. That big heart, combined with her intellect and self-belief, quickly took her from university (BA and MA) to a top-level career in the media. By the age of twenty-six, Princess was an editor on the state television evening news programme. This exalted post promised great things for Princess. It allowed her to exhibit all her skills; intelligence, charm, humour and style. Her family were delighted, especially her father, who took this as confirmation of his princess's unique qualities.

Within two years, Princess was Senior Editor and heading upwards.

Then a change happened. She was head-hunted by a newly-established, well-financed, private TV company. The post was Head of Film Channel. Princess couldn't resist the opportunity and eagerly signed the contract.

So far, so promising, though that career move was unexpected. Anyone who'd become a Princess-watcher might now be wondering why she would move so quickly from a secure, upwardly mobile career with state TV to the more performative work culture of private television.

Princess merely told her friends and family what they expected to hear, which was the private TV company were offering her a better contract; higher salary, more autonomy, and better prospects of promotion.

The truth was more complex. Princess had yet to find an organisational environment that would indulge her sense of entitlement, ego and pride and she hoped the private television company might do just that.

She was just twenty-eight.

Husband No. 1

Princess not only found exciting work at the TV station, she also found a husband. He was a senior manager, the same age as her, and he too was on the way to the top. They made the perfect power couple and were married after a brief courtship.

At this point, the story of Princess takes a sharp turn downwards, for within twelve months she was divorced.

Whatever passion existed between Princess and her Prince Charming ended within weeks of the marriage, though not before she'd become pregnant. That act of conception was one of the last times she had sex for many years. She found sex with her husband unpleasant if not painful. Her husband, did not, which was partly the reason he began an affair with another media colleague during Princess's pregnancy. The other reason was that he didn't consider Princess to be royalty. He loved her style and had fallen for her glamour and charm. But he was never going to dote on her. He found paying homage too high a price.

By the time her son was born, Princess was already looking for a new career move. The thought of returning to her job in the TV company, having to work alongside her ex-husband and his girlfriend, was not something any princess could seriously consider.

She was just thirty-one. So far, following her heart had proven risky if not disastrous. Her ego was bruised, her pride was severely damaged, and the future looked a lot more uncertain.

However, she was still a Princess and princesses must be indulged otherwise what's the point?

More Moves

Having worked for the top two state and private television companies in her country in the space of just five years, and left each after only two years, Princess had a dilemma. Where next?

The media still attracted her – she liked the glamour, networking with powerful people, and the creative challenges it offered. She opted for newspapers.

Over the next five years Princess worked in two leading newspapers, first as a feature editor and then as a senior news editor. Her salary is lower than the television companies provided, but she continues to be financially independent and able to pay for quality childcare for her growing son.

However, one lesson Princess is having to learn is that it is okay to consider yourself a special woman but not okay to expect special treatment from work colleagues, the majority of whom are your equal in terms of intelligence and ability. And this is especially so in the macho world of newspaper publishing. While Princess enjoys being seen as 'one of the team', the fact is she is female and therefore considered an outsider in this male dominated world. When her male colleagues flock off to the bars after work, Princess doesn't get invited and anyway, she must hurry home to her child.

There is no special treatment for Princess and certainly no idolisation, at least not at work. Princess has a big ego but it is fragile. It requires constantly to be puffed up. She is too susceptible to praise and too susceptible to criticism. To be sure, Princess is resilient but only on the surface. Deep down inside she is insecure; requiring constant praise and being afraid of criticism signals vulnerability.

Princess is a lot more vulnerable than she appears on the surface.

Husband No. 2

Despite her rather disrupted and disruptive career trajectory, life is looking up on the personal side. Princess has met a highly desirable man. He is classy and handsome, five years older than her, a doctor with his own private medical practice and a lecturer at the country's top medical university. The fact that he is divorced and has a daughter from that marriage, doesn't deter Princess. Her head and her heart both tell her this is the man to ensure she remains on the pedestal. Moreover, Princesses must have a palace, and her second husband can afford one.

In pursuit of excellence in all aspects of her life, Princess becomes obsessed with her beautiful new family home. Her pride in her professional status remains but now she has the resources to turn her home into that palace. This must be the model family and Princess expends much energy and time on ensuring the house is always spotlessly clean, that organic food fills the fridge and freezer, and that her son and step-daughter look pristine on their way to their international school.

Within six months, that family home has a new arrival – a baby boy.

Looking back, this is the apex of Princess's life, at least so far. She literally has everything she could possibly desire. Sure, there are one or two clouds on the horizon, the darkest being her mother-in-law who turns out to be extremely hostile towards Princess. But no matter, her husband loves her unconditionally, her home is magnificent, the children are happy and healthy, and her job ensures her financial independence. This is Princess's perfection plateau.

Aged thirty-seven, Princess has finally made the transition from becoming a princess to being one.

The Wounding Years

The catalogue of disasters that now start to rain down on Princess is almost too large to detail. But the next decade of her life is a time of desperate pain and despair for this proud, capable and intelligent woman. As a Buddhist, Princess believes in karma, but even she cannot comprehend why she should have to suffer such outrageous misfortune, with every year seemingly bringing her more stress, more emotional turmoil and more diminishment of her self-esteem.

> *"Did the gods plan all that for me? Did they look at my life and my expectations and decide to bring me down a few notches? I don't know but I certainly came down with a crash. I've not yet got back up again."*

The wounding years of Princess's life began with betrayal. Her husband's.

> *"When I met him he'd just finished a long relationship with a woman who subsequently went to China for a year, to work. Then she came back and he renewed the affair almost immediately. We'd been married about a year."*

That particular affair of her husband's continues for many years, though it's not his only sexual betrayal of Princess.

> *"His private clinic operation brings him into contact with many women. How many has he slept with? I've no idea, but it must be a great many."*

Throughout her life, Princess has felt competitive with other women, especially those with beauty and brains. She now finds herself in the desperate situation of being rejected by her husband, sexually, while he embarks on serial sexual escapades. For any woman to be so treated is painful; for Princess it is inconceivable.

To add to her misery, her husband starts to spend time away from home. He has set up a second home with his previous, long-time girlfriend. His neglect of the family puts additional pressure on Princess. She has three young children to raise and finds herself having to do so without the moral and practical support of their father.

The next blow to Princess came from her most treasured love – her father. When her youngest son was just two years old, her father was diagnosed with skin cancer and the prognosis was bad. He had months to live. In fact, he lived for another two years, but throughout that time Princess had to endure his slow demise and carry the burden of providing emotional support for her mother.

> *"My father was my true support in life. He had always been there for me. To lose him was the most terrible blow. It added to my loneliness and feeling of being isolated."*

By this point, Princess is starting to doubt herself. She may be a princess and special, but she'd always believed that if a woman is good, both as wife and homemaker, then her husband will love her, be faithful to her and that all the family, including her in-laws, will respect and love her. In other words, the future of the family and the home inevitably rested on the shoulders of the wife and mother.

In Princess's mind, and following such gendered logical thinking, she must therefore be held responsible for the problems in her marriage.

That self-doubt deepens when an incident at work spurs her to embark on yet another career move, this time into education.

> *"The newspaper office culture was always highly competitive. The guys tended to stick together and the few women had to do the same. Unfortunately, a woman colleague and I fell out badly over a feature editing decision I had made, and that left me feeling stressed and insecure. I decided to quit."*

The accumulation of difficulties is causing Princess health issues. She is not sleeping well, she is stressed and she feels depressed. But she still needs to earn a living. Maybe it is time she left the hothouse culture of the media profession and enter an altogether calmer work environment – university lecturing.

> *"With my media background and qualifications, it wasn't too difficult for me to get a lectureship in a good university. I did that job for two years. Why did I leave? I got bored with it. I didn't find the education profession particularly inspiring after being in the media. And then I got an offer to work as magazine editor."*

While all this is going on in Princess's life, her mother-in-law adds to her anguish.

> "She and I just never got on. She is always angry with me, always frustrated, unhappy and hostile. She is quick-tempered. She hasn't the patience to look after children so I have to pay for childcare. She knows about by husband's affairs, but ignores them. She blames me."

Princess, now aged forty-two, is only half-way through her worst-ever decade. She still has more to suffer.

> "The magazine editor job didn't work out for me. I didn't have any real status and the pay wasn't that good. The best thing about media is the creative element but for that you need space to think and work. I didn't have it. I was exhausted all the time. I still am. Just holding the family together mostly by myself took a real toll on my health, my wellbeing."

Since she graduated from her MA at the age of twenty-five, Princess has had seven jobs in four different professional arenas: TV, newspapers, higher education and magazines. Unfortunately, this career pattern has not led to higher pay and higher positions. In fact, she is now earning less than she did after graduation.

> "I've been working in the state system too long and now it's difficult to get out. My current job, which I've had for five years, is as editor for a state-run magazine. The job is secure but I don't have the prestige of working in television. I have no prospects of promotion. Nor do I have a good income."

Whatever pride and arrogance Princess once had is now eliminated. She has come a long way in her life, but not in the direction she imagined when she was eighteen. There are moments, periods in her life, when she had it all, only to lose it twice as fast.

Her choice in men is one problem. Princess has had lots of male admirers but she is no seductress. She doesn't even enjoy sex that much, which is just as well because she has been celibate since she discovered her husband's affairs. The two men she has had in her life became her husbands but stuck around only for a short time before sexually betraying her. She has remained married to her second husband but that is because she cannot afford to get divorced.

"I have tried to pressure my husband to give up the affairs, stop drinking, spend more time with me and the children, but his response is always to say he gives me money every month so what more do I want?"

But the biggest problem for Princess is not so apparent as choosing the wrong husband. It is to do with her poor self-awareness. This feeds her toxic femininity which in turn holds her back from making the really crucial changes in her life.

Transformation

The crux of Princess's problem is captured in this statement:

"I want my life to be perfect. What is wrong with that? And I have nearly achieved that perfection at times over the past two decades. It is not my fault my husbands were unfaithful or my work colleagues spiteful and jealous."

Lives are never lived in isolation. We all connect, we all belong and we all contribute. But the quality and depth of our connection with others corresponds with the quality and depth of our connection with ourselves. Our external relationships mirror our internal relationship. Princess lacks that inner connection. She is unreflective and obsessed with appearing perfect, powerful and successful. This leaves her living her life on the surface only. She is shallow.

Princess's toxic femininity contains five key elements which interrupt the possibility of her connecting, belonging and contributing in a fair, harmonious, healthy and positive way.

1. The absence of reflection. In Princess's case she fails to accept her failures, fails to recognise the gendered circumstances which have informed her life, and therefore is unable to see beyond the immediate situation she finds herself in.

2. Emotional Mismanagement: In Princess's case that means denying negative emotions in herself (shame, fear, envy, jealousy) and identifying with those emotions which she feels bolster her ego, power and self-esteem (disdain, loathing, hate, rage, anger).

3. Gendered Pride. In Princess's case, she always believed she was better than other women. And in her early life, she was, at least in the speed of her career advancement. But when her life went

sour that pride turned to shame when comparing herself with other women.

4. Needing to Be Number One: In Princess's case, the joy of being the 'princess' became a deadly trap because one day she was no longer number one. She was then forced to accept being inferior, at least by her own mental self-assessment.

5. Problem Projection: In Princess's case, her go-to position when faced with problems is to expect others to change; she cannot change herself. As far her career is concerned, one small criticism has proved enough for her to quit her job on many occasions. She wants to be seen as better than her colleagues, but instead ends up being defeated by one simple word.

These unresolved tensions in Princess's life accumulated to the point that she eventually crashed off her pedestal. Many people did indeed treat her badly, not least her two husbands, but then she also treated herself badly. There was plenty of toxicity in Princess's life, but a lot of it came from within her. If people have tried to pull her down off her pedestal, Princess's own behaviours and actions helped them do so.

Despite all this misfortune, a large slice of it the result of Princess's own attitude and behaviour, fate did have one more trick to play on her. Thankfully, it was a nice trick.

As Princess was to discover, the remedy to the torment and anguish in her life did not lie with others; it lay within herself.

The Princess of Sonnets

As is revealed in most of the stories in this book, when a woman reaches the pit of despair and depression she often realises there is only one way to go and that is up – even if the climb is going to be pretty unpleasant, it's more pleasant than staying put. Such is the case with Princess. Unfortunately, Princess's 'upward year' happened to be a testing year for all of humanity – 2020. Covid-19 had begun decimating economies, communities and families. What this virus meant for Princess was not just physical isolation with her children (her husband now living with his girlfriend), it meant unemployment, financial hardship and acute mental stress.

"I was barely coping as it was then Covid hit my country. The magazine cut back on staff and I was made temporarily redundant. I was living off a pittance, with only the small amount of money my

husband gave me every month to get by on. My health was bad, with severe chest pains due to anxiety. The one thing I did have was a good circle of friends, many of them in the medical profession. I saw the pressure they were under due to Covid and I found it inspiring. That is what started it."

It was while she was experiencing her greatest sense of loss, hopelessness and self-pity, that Princess found a jewel. That jewel was her ability to write about her feelings. At the beginning it was merely a form of self-therapy, but it quickly grew into something even more rewarding.

"It was one of those days when my three children had gone to stay overnight with their father and his girlfriend. I was listening to some music and the words of the song resonated with how I was feeling. But the song didn't capture all of it for me, there was an element missing. I decided to try and write my own song. Actually, it started as a poem and grew into a sonnet. I didn't think it was anything special but I showed it to a close woman friend, an expert on literature, and she thought it was good and encouraged me to continue. Once I started, I couldn't stop."

Having unlocked the door to her own feelings, recognising them, embracing them, and owning them, so Princess's writing grew more beautiful and more powerful.

"My first published sonnet was not about myself, but about my heroic doctor friends, having to deal with Covid-19 and all the death and despair the virus was causing for them and for all of us. They were amazing and I felt someone should write something and acknowledge that."

Many people like to write, to put their feelings and thoughts down on paper, but few have the confidence to seek publication. Princess did have that confidence. One thing Princess never lacked was self-appreciation.

Princess sent her first sonnet off to an online magazine which duly published it. The response was amazing. People loved the words she wrote, the way she expressed her fears, hopes and her gratitude to the medical profession in her country.

"I was overwhelmed by the response. It took me by surprise. Gave me a real lift. Made me feel so much more positive. I just carried on writing and getting work published."

While Princess was not making a living out of this writing, she was getting known. Within weeks she became nationally famous. She even had her own poetry page in a popular women's online magazine. Because these were sonnets (long poems) they suited a lot of musicians and many of them took her writings and turned them into songs. Her sonnets became a feature of popular culture.

For the first time in her life, Princess could truly consider herself to be special. Why? Because other people were saying so. She had discovered deep within herself the capacity for emotional expression, but in a positive and creative way. Her words were nurturing, emotive, insightful and subtle; they came from her beautiful soul and connected with other beautiful souls.

During the Covid epidemic, a time of fear, loneliness and dreadful anxiety, people found solace in Princess's sonnets.

The Princess of Sonnets had finally realised her place in the world – in the palace of wordsmiths.

Where Is She Now?

After Covid-19 declined, Princess returned to work full-time for the state magazine. Her husband finally left his girlfriend and moved back into the family home. Their three children are all heading for university. The family finances are healthier, though Princess is unlikely to ever be wealthy.

Princess has taken the knocks and the falls, and has the bruises to prove it. Her ego and pride have been given a thorough going over during the past decade. She is no longer the entitled, unreflective, self-regarding woman of her youth. Princess has had to grow up but in the process she's also grown old, and it shows. The endless storms have taken their toll on her health and her beauty though not on her spirit – that remains strong and indeed she has far more inner resilience than ever before. The process of writing has proved immensely therapeutic, enjoyable and satisfying for Princess. She has received national recognition. However, her life experiences have made her wary of using all this attention to puff up her ego.

> "I've been in the media a long time and I know how fast people forget. My songs and sonnets are being read and listened to by millions, but I wrote them for myself and for those I felt deserved to be recognized for what they were doing for society, that is, the medical profession in my country. So whether or not the sonnets continue to get published, I won't stop writing. I've discovered something within myself that I never knew existed. But it took a lot of pain and loneliness before I could reach it."

Overcoming Toxic Femininity

Princess has been both a victim and perpetrator of toxic femininity. As a daughter-in-law she was a victim. Her mother-in-law's emotional violence towards her caused so much unnecessary pain and anguish for Princess. At precisely that time when Princess really needed support from her mother-in-law regarding her husband's serial infidelities and emotional abuse, she was denied it. There was to be no sense of sisterhood between these two women, only accusation, judgement and harsh bitter words.

The toxic femininity that Princess expresses is less coarse and explicit than that shown by her mother-in-law. It is revealed in her sense of entitlement; convinced she should have it all and therefore should be treated exclusively and exceptionally. It is revealed in her inability to accept criticism and needing constant praise from all those around her. One bad word from a work colleague would be enough for Princess to start looking for another job. It is revealed in her sense of competition towards other women. She doesn't see other women, many of whom suffer in bad marriages just like hers, as sisters. She had no empathy and little emotional management – her pride and arrogance got in the way of all that. It is revealed in her failure to accept her own part in her downfall. Too quick to blame others, she never got close to reflecting on her actions. And it is revealed in her lack of self-awareness. Self-appreciation without self-awareness is unlikely to lead to self-development.

In effect, the very concept of this woman as a princess created a trap into which she duly fell. Her sense of entitlement, combined with a competitive mindset and pride but lack of resilience in the face of criticism, created a dangerous imbalance in her sense of self. There was no possibility of healthy self-love in Princess because it got blocked by her zero self-sufficiency.

Princess cannot yet claim to have fully overcome her toxic femininity but she has made remarkable progress. Having almost accidentally become a writer, she now finds the writing has a balming and consoling effect on her wounded ego and diminished pride. Through the writing so is she discovering herself; revealing the woman who exists below the shallow surface onto which she previously projected so much of her self-worth. In order to write these sonnets, Princess must pay minute attention to her negative emotions, the ones she previously denied in herself; that is acutely therapeutic. The sonnets reveal her light and dark sides, and also her inner beauty, not least to herself. In this way, so does the writing open a door to her inner world. She now connects with herself in a positive way, no longer requiring validation through having power over and feeling superior to others, especially women. She becomes calmer, more joyful, more contented, but also more accepting of weaknesses in others as well as in herself. She begins to see beyond her own desires and expectations. In accumulating this inner power, she can now connect healthily with the outer world.

In truth, Princess can never stop writing or creating sonnets; the process is her lifebelt and she can never let go. Fame, artistic recognition, and an improved social and emotional life are her new sources of joy and excitement. She started out writing in order to ameliorate inner pain. Not only did she achieve that, but she found a new and powerful ego boost due to the success she achieved. Princess's ego has not disappeared, but nowadays she can get that ego boost in a healthy way, via writing words that bring comfort and pleasure to others, not from attempting to be the number one person in the building.

Princess has embarked on a journey of redemption. Her poems, sonnets and songs have touched the hearts and minds of millions and given her enormous pleasure and satisfaction. The storms will continue to rage in her life, especially in her marriage, though nowadays she has greater resources to weather them.

While her identity remains fragile, Princess is acquiring inner strength and resilience, she is less driven by ego and more by empathetic appreciation for those around her. She draws great comfort from her writing and every time she hears one of her sonnets being performed, she really does feel like the princess she's always been.

When the little leaf
Owns
Her inner storm

She owns
All the torrential rains
All the relentless winds
All the bombardment of hails...

And the whole jungle
Turns
Tranquil...

Chapter Ten: Poet

Memories Are Made of This

One of the traits required to survive a marriage is a short memory: that and the ability to let go of hurt and anger. Those of us blessed, or rather cursed, with a long memory and the inability to easily forget what was said or done in the heat of the moment are condemned to suffer the emotional trauma over and over again. Not being able to let go means we will be reliving that argument, that pain, in our heads for some time to come.

Of course, it can also be important not to forget what was said and done to us, nor what we said and did in return. Because all these episodes count: they all contribute to the sum total of our life experience. They all inform the journey. It follows that these experiences help form us and help make us who we are. But this more philosophical perspective is only of benefit if we learn from our experiences, both the good and the bad. If all we do is simply remember but never learn and never reflect, then for sure we will end up reliving these situations not just in our minds but in our future lives. It is largely up to us whether that life will be a Groundhog Day or a Sound of Music.

Poet's life started out as the Sound of Music, but then became a Groundhog Day. As you read through her fascinating story you too may hope that the music is returning to her life.

A Good Start

None of us gets to choose our parents, which means we have no influence on how our life begins. But if we do get to choose, then Poet is one of those who chose well. She grew up in a stable, close-knit, loving and kind-hearted family environment. She was given all the care and attention any child could wish for plus space to become the woman she aspired to be. Poet was pretty, slim and artistic. While her female friends drooled over with the latest pop star, Poet was writing and painting.

This good start continued through university, where she studied in a leading university of education, training to become a teacher of arts.

Although her family were not poor, neither were they rich, so when Poet graduated and was subsequently appointed as a teacher, life looked rosier than ever.

One of her fellow students, himself an artist, caught Poet's eye. He was handsome, popular, and suggestively masculine. They started dating in their final year. This perfect student romance was perfectly complemented by financial security. For what Poet didn't know was that her fiancé's family owned valuable residential land in the city. When the couple got married, at the age of twenty-five, the family provided land on which to build the most beautiful home. Poet had her secure teaching job while her husband was now a stage design artist for a touring theatre group. Their joint income, combined with Poet's artistic temperament, meant they could design and furnish their home to the envy of all who knew them.

Poet's good fortune continued for another seven years, until the age of thirty-two. By then she had a delightful six-year old daughter and a new-born son.

The first turning point in Poet's life came during the birth of her son. Complications meant this was a near-death experience for her and for her new baby. Although Poet recovered, she suffered continuing exhaustion and post-natal depression.

Unfortunately, this period coincided with another family crisis – her husband's salary plummeted. A global recession reduced his salary to a fraction; in effect putting him out of work. There were no touring stage groups and therefore no need for stage designers.

Gone were the warm sunny days of good fortune and plenty. Gone was the luck.

Dark Clouds and Lightning

No one seeks a hard life. No one wants the curse of misfortune. And only the masochistic like pain. But life doesn't care. We all get something of the negative along with the positive, like it or not. Every life has its dark clouds and lightning, and Poet now had hers.

The dark clouds were the family's growing money problems and her incessant tiredness. The traumatic childbirth had left her physically fragile and with low blood pressure. But Poet's will remained strong and she never gave up. She was determined to give the kind of love to her kids that her family had given to her. It helped that Poet had a secure teaching job, but childcare duties meant she had to reduce to part-time. The family finances got even tighter.

The lightning was the twin fork type.

The first fork of lightning was a mother-in-law who had always looked down on Poet because she came from a poorer family. Now she turned toxic. Although the mother-in-law helped Poet with the childcare, she took to being highly judgemental, emotionally branding Poet 'useless' and 'lazy'.

The second fork of lightning was her husband – he succumbed to alcoholism.

One of the few, if important, benefits of strife and struggle when we are young is that it can prepare us for tough times as adults. We can learn to cope. Poet could not cope. Nothing in her cloudless, blue-sky young life prepared her for where life was now heading. Her artistic, sensitive nature combined with a repetitive memory, made it almost impossible to let go of harsh words from her mother-in-law and the drunken abuse of her husband.

Day upon day of bitter comments came to infect Poet's mind and diminish her self-confidence, leaving a scar on her heart. She lost weight, became depressed and found it hard to find hope in anything. There was to be no solace in her artistic activities – those ceased completely – nor joy in her marriage; the sheer effort of keeping the family together put paid to all that. She was now, effectively, on her own, trapped in circumstances she could not possibly have foreseen.

That beautiful house was to become her beautiful prison.

With her husband the prison tormentor.

Being a stage designer was a well-paid job when the theatres were open, but it had its drawbacks. One drawback was frequently being away from home and spending evenings drinking in bars with other members of the group. When her husband had his job, his drinking was not so much of a problem. He had money, a regular occupation, and a lot of self-respect.

All that ended with unemployment. Alcohol filled the vacuum in his life. By the time his son was aged two, Poet's husband was drunk every day and most of the day. Fortunately for Poet and the children, he preferred to drink in the local bars rather than at home. But even the bars closed, at which point Poet's day of struggle and weariness became a night of abuse and torment.

Their meagre family income was barely enough to buy food, let alone beer and whisky. The debts started to accumulate. In a wretched state, Poet had no choice but to beg her mother-in-law for financial help. She received it, though this reluctantly given largesse only served to make Poet's relationship with her in-law even more unpleasant.

The Dustbin

For a decade, Poet suffered this situation. The family still had the beautiful home, but they were living in poverty. They may have looked rich on the outside, but behind closed doors the home-life was desperate. Her mother-in-law's toxic femininity scarred Poet's life, while her husband's drunkenness dramatically added to her emotional poverty. Once her son was old enough for school, Poet was able to return to her full-time teaching job, but surviving on one income was not easy. Those years of hardship and isolation gathered in her mind.

> "I couldn't let go of the suffering I'd endured and was still having to cope with. It built up in my memory and stayed there. My marriage was really over but divorce was out of the question in my family, my culture. My home was in my husband's family name, not mine. I was stuck."

Poet absorbed all the cruel words and hardship and then deposited it in her memory. By the age of forty-two, that memory was like a full dustbin storing all the toxicity thrown at her by her mother-in-law and husband. She was tortured by how her life had changed, how it had gone sour. The pain in her heart created agony in her mind.

Poet was cursed with an excellent memory. Nothing got forgotten. Not the time her mother-in-law slapped her in the face, the many times she insulted her, swore at her. Nor the countless occasions her drunken husband came home shouting, calling her a whore, smashing up the home. Both her husband and his mother repeated the same accusations to Poet; that of being useless, nothing, worthless.

Poet remembered all this. Nothing got forgotten, which meant that no one got forgiven.

But she at least had a job.

Perversely that made things worse for Poet. Being a teacher could be stressful at times and when she was back home, trying to rest, her mind was in overload. In the rare moments she could get some time to herself, her memory was free to do its work and what it did was bring up bad situations from the past. Constantly.

The depression that Poet had suffered after the birth of her son now resurfaced but more seriously. She was diagnosed and given medication to help her sleep and relax.

> *"The pills gave me a headache and made me very sleepy. I felt myself changing in my personality. They relaxed me but also left me heavy in my brain. I could see myself putting on weight and becoming addicted to the pills. So I stopped taking them."*

Stopping the medication helped Poet maintain her lithe figure and pretty face, but it did nothing for her depression. That she would have to cure on her own.

> *"Looking back, I don't know how I got through those first ten years of my son's life. I was married but really living on my own, in my own head. Work at least got me out of the house, and my husband would take himself off drinking every night, sometimes be gone for a few days at a time. I didn't care what he did as long as he left me and the children in peace. I found some moments of peace but they were few. There were no joys in my life, other than my children who were growing up fine. I devoted myself to them. That was all I cared about. I didn't care about myself."*

Poet has now reached the first of her rock-bottoms.

A Way Up

If you aim to move from a past that is torturing you then you must first start with a present which is at least a little bit hopeful. Letting go of hurt may not necessarily require you to forget, but it does require you to become less absorbed in the past and more involved in the here and now.

This was a challenge for Poet, because she continued to live with the main tormentor in her life – her husband. Every day was, for Poet, a visible reminder of her husband's failings, and her failings as a wife; being unable to do much about the grim situation in which she been living now for over ten years was, she believed, her burden to carry.

As she saw it, her life was satisfactory only in one area – being a mother. Her determination to keep the family together, financially and emotionally, had paid off. Both children were growing up as fine as could be expected under the circumstances and were heading for university. However, very soon neither child would need their mother in quite the way they had.

Financially, the family were just about coping, as long as Poet kept her job, which looked likely.

And what of Poet's intimate life? Where had that gone? Inevitably, it had disappeared. She and her husband no longer had an intimate life. Sex between them was a distant memory – this was one memory that Poet cared not to reflect on. She was happy to be celibate. Nevertheless, she knew she was missing something, just not sure what.

Mother, wife, teacher: three key identities for Poet but all, in one way or another, either dysfunctional or failing to fulfil her inner essence as a woman. That left the artist.

The breakthrough came when a friend got married and Poet had to make herself a dress for the wedding. She couldn't afford to buy one. Poet applied all her artistic skills into creating a most beautiful dress for herself, so much so that at the wedding several of her friends asked where she'd bought it. She proudly told them it was her creation. Thereafter, Poet was never without a job making similarly beautiful dresses for her friends. Not for the income it gave her, which was little, but for the sheer joy and satisfaction of nurturing once again her artistic identity.

This additional occupation allowed Poet to escape the memories, free herself from regret, guilt, and inadequacy and focus on herself. Life became a lot more enjoyable and certainly more satisfying. Indeed, the moment when a dress was finished and presented to its proud owner, was actually quite exciting. Poet started to feel good about herself. And feeling good about herself was a welcome improvement in her life. The toxic femininity she had absorbed during her marriage manifested itself in a feeling of worthlessness. Now she had the means to challenge it. These beautiful dresses were not worthless and she had created them. Ergo, she wasn't as worthless as she'd imagined.

Here was a way up from rock bottom and Poet took it.

The Shaman

One of the conditions of toxic femininity is that it makes a woman believe she is of little value unless loved by a man. In other words, whatever love she has to give, she gives to him, not to herself.

The danger this poses to lonely and hurting women is obvious – because need overwhelms good judgement.

Poet was now at risk.

To be sure, now in her forty-fifth year, Poet's life was more promising. Her job was going well, she was making beautiful dresses for appreciative friends, the children were in higher education and beginning their own adult lives, while her husband spent most of his time out with his pals or sleeping it off in the spare bedroom. Her toxic mother-in-law was old and infirm and therefore could be easily ignored. Poet felt she was getting her life back.

But a vacuum remained. And, ironically, the more hopeful she became about the future, her future, the bigger that vacuum became.

That vacuum was love and desire. But while this need and yearning got stronger within Poet, her self-love was not improving. She was still an attractive woman, but inside she did not feel attractive at all. She could not see how any man would be interested in her.

Like most women of her age, Poet had discovered social media and was enjoying the communicative possibilities it offered. Not that Poet ever considered dating or finding a man online. She was far too traditional, modest and decent for that. What she was interested in was spirituality.

It didn't take long for Poet to discover spiritual, Buddhist and meditation communities online. And nor did it take long for her to meet the Shaman.

The Shaman presented himself as a spiritual Guru. In his home town, some 300 km from where Poet lived, he appeared to be respected, active in leading prayer meetings and meditations, and even presiding over weddings and other communal events. He had a vibrant and growing online community, spread around the country.

Poet had always had spiritual feelings but her years of hardship had dampened them. Now she felt possibilities open up. She wanted to nurture herself, mindfully and metaphysically. But where to start? None of the concepts around spirituality and Buddhism were familiar to Poet. She was a novice.

The Shaman stepped in.

Within weeks, Poet and the Shaman were communicating online daily, sometimes many times a day. She had lots of opportunity at work to chat with the Shaman and alone in her bedroom at night: saying goodnight to him became her last act before sleep.

She was asking question – she was the student. The Shaman was answering those questions – the expert, the tutor. He was a sage, counsellor, teacher and mentor, all wrapped in a very good-looking, if not virile, masculine package.

Here was a man in touch with his inner feelings. He had answers to so many of Poet's dilemmas. He was articulate, confident, knowing, kind and warm. He was also a non-drinker, which Poet found especially appealing. She is mesmerised by his wisdom and by his worldly-knowledge. He seems to understand her like no one has ever done. She feels he knows her better than she knows herself.

Poet quickly falls in love.

The online romance deepens over one summer. And becomes sexual. Encouraged by the Shaman to trust him and feel safe, Poet shares intimate photos of herself. Poet is not having sex with the Shaman, in fact they never physically meet, but she is experiencing some satisfaction. Part of her need for physical intimacy is being met. She feels desired, wanted, beautiful and – for the first time in many years – feminine.

That summer of love is the most romantic Poet had ever experienced. The fact that she is, in her mind, middle-aged and plain, only makes the encounter more poignant and meaningful.

And then, the inevitable happens. Poet wakes up one morning eager to read the latest message from her online Shaman lover, only to find a message from another woman.

> "The message was very simple, it said: 'Don't trust this man. He has many, many women online just like you.' At first, I didn't believe her. But curiosity got the better of me and I replied to her. She showed me photos he had sent her, naked photos of himself. And she showed me his messages to her. She gave me other women to contact who'd also been seduced by him. There were many. I was devastated. All my dreams crashed immediately. What a fool I had been."

This second rock bottom proved to be even deeper than the first.

> "I was actually grieving. I was mad with pain. I just couldn't stop thinking about what had happened to me. Why did I deserve all this? I had trusted my husband and he had let me down. Now I had trusted only the second man in my life and he'd done the same. I felt all the emotions but I especially felt dirty. Not just the photos but because I still needed him, was missing him."

The love affair may have been solely acted out online but that didn't make it any less real for Poet. For anyone who falls in love online, it still feels like falling in love. The force and power of the emotion can be overwhelming – overwhelmingly beautiful and overwhelmingly painful if it ends badly.

As Poet discovered, the emotional pain of Shaman's 'infidelity' cut her as traumatically as any knife could.

Nothing in Poet's life had prepared her for this. She was one of life's innocents: a woman who had grown up protected by a loving, secure family now found herself alone among predators in a very confusing and dangerous world.

Broken

Whatever pain and despair Poet had suffered in her marriage somehow seemed less traumatic than this betrayal by Shaman. Poet truly imagined she had at last found a mature love, a stable kind man whom she could trust with all her secrets and needs.

This emotional wound to Poet was heightened by her sensitive and artistic nature. She had the capacity to see beauty in the mundane and ordinary. And she saw beauty in this man. It was not difficult to fall in love with Shaman – she took his words and turned them into an image that she found desirable and trusting. She projected her deep needs and insecurities onto this online face and, confident she was having her needs reciprocated, not surprisingly, fell in love with it.

Shaman was false and duplicitous for sure, but Poet was also unwise and inexperienced.

As so often in such situations, the crisis of a spurned love became a crisis of self-significance – Poet felt no significance. She felt nothing, only emptiness.

Her heart was broken.

> "There are no words to describe how I felt at that time. I was lost, broken up. What did I have left in my life – for me? No one needed me as a woman. I couldn't see any future."

Poet had now reached the depths. There was no music playing in her life, only an endless loop of shame, regret and hurtfulness repeating itself in her memory, drowning out all hope.

Groundhog Day.

Rebirth

The rebirthing of Poet began one morning, in the university library. A woman university lecturer got chatting with Poet about poetry; they both shared a love of romantic and spiritual poems. Poet happened to say that she wrote poems and the two women struck up what was to become a very close and lasting friendship.

Poet had written verses when she was young, but stopped through her marriage. She'd restarted with Shaman.

Shaman may have given Poet pain, but at least he got her writing again.

Encouraged by her new friend, Poet began to turn her heartache into something more productive – poignant words of love won and lost.

And then she took it even further – she turned to photography.

"I was out walking in my local park one evening, it was dusk, I sat on a bench and just looked at the sky. The clouds had somehow formed themselves into a heart shape. I took a photo on my mobile phone. When I got home I posted it on social media. Loads of people liked it. That was the start of my photography hobby."

The sensitive, artistic, romantic side of Poet now blossomed. Poetry and photography became her first loves. She found solace in verse and photographic images of sunbeams, budding flowers and blue horizons.

Poet had always had beauty inside her – it had never gone away. But her life experiences had hidden it so deep she could no longer find it. Indeed, she thought she had lost it forever.

But within her inner sanctuary of self, down in her very soul, beauty remained. It hadn't died. All those years of toxic, sour memories, all the heartache and disappointment had not erased the most important aspects of Poet – her caring, tender, artistic character.

She had never become bitter and angry, only deeply saddened within herself.

"Poetry and photography have given me the opportunity for self-expression. They free my mind from going over all the rubbish that has happened to me since I was in my early thirties. When I am writing a poem or taking photographs, I am not remembering the bad years. I am in the moment. I did learn something from Shaman and that was to be in the moment. I've come to realise that my hobbies, poetry and photography not only produce something special to me, they produce something of beauty. It is actually quite meditative. Peaceful."

A sole candle
far away
in the jungle's night

My loneliness
quivers
In the winter's cold

(Poet)

How Did Poet Make the Transformation?

Poet was broken and needed to be rebuilt. Only she could do that; no one else, man or woman, could do it for her. Being broken is traumatic but it is also a chance to rebuild oneself. Poet put her broken pieces back together again, but this time the final construction was stronger, more robust and much healthier, both physically and mentally.

This is how she did it:

1. Acceptance and Forgiveness

1.   She escaped from the tornado of emotions by distinguishing between pain over feeling betrayed by Shaman, pain over her shame, and pain over her continued craving for him.

2.   She recognised she was addicted to Shaman, to the excitement he brought into her life and that this was a weakness she needed to deal with. She was then able to recognise her self-loathing (for wanting more of him).

3.   She came to accept who she was as a woman, that the desires and needs she had for intimacy and love were natural and should be cared for and accepted. This way she reduced her feelings of guilt, shame and self-loathing.

4.   She forgave him in her mind and in her memory. She recognised his own weaknesses and had no malice for him. In her mind she replaced anger for Shaman with sympathy for Shaman.

2. Being Kind to Herself

1.   She practised saying good and nurturing things to herself. She made this a daily routine.

2.   She tolerated her weaknesses and accepted her mental and physical needs.

3.   She practised being aware of her emotions and transformed them when she could.

4.   She used her poetry as a form of self-talk, an outlet for her acute, often painful memories and emotions.

5.   She indulged herself by taking time out for her dressmaking, writing and photography.

6.   She prioritised her needs, especially rest, exercise and her hobbies.

3. Communicating Herself to Others

1.   She described her nuanced emotions on social media and felt consoled and comforted when people commented and liked them.

2.   She used social media as a mental tonic, a comforting zone where she felt able to express herself safely to friends.

3.   She opened up her heart to close friends on a one-to-one, and accepted advice when given. She used these more intimate conversations to explore herself and her reactions to situations and painful memories.

4.   She came to recognise that many of her women friends had also experienced pain and disappointment in their lives, especially in relationships. This helped build within her a feeling of shared experience with other women.

5.   The kindness and empathy she gave to other women was in turn given to her. Her loneliness lessened remarkably.

4. Living in the Now

1.   She learned to stop the cruel replay of bad memories in her brain and heart by focusing on the beauty of the present; a tiny flower, a floating cloud, the fragrance of a flower, the subtle change from day to night, the empty street through a window on a rainy day.

2.   She allowed herself to get lost in the beauty all around her and thus escape from the prison of the past. She stopped being a mere dustbin.

3.   She used poetry and photography to capture the everyday beauty which surrounded her.

4.   She used dressmaking to give something back to her women friends.

This transformation did not happen overnight, but it was progressively beneficial to all aspects of her – mental and physical. The depth of Poet's heartache had manifested itself as bad health and exhaustion. She was in constant pain in her stomach. But as each day went by so she grew stronger, more confident and more determined. Her artistic nature was a powerful weapon to win over her devastation. Slowly but surely, the pain reduced, as did her stress levels.

Persisting with this slow transformation, Poet gathered momentum and improved her mindset. She transformed herself from a depressed and self-loathing woman to a proud, contented and happy one. Poet became an emotional warrior. Every minor victory was a battle won and every battle won told her she would eventually win this war.

Where Is She Now?

If life has any purpose then perhaps it is self-discovery. From the moment of birth, we are learning, acquiring knowledge and – hopefully – understanding, not least about ourselves, our strengths, weaknesses and possibilities. But to do so we must accept and learn to live with disappointment, regret, rejection and trauma. Not easy, but then, this is what makes life truly meaningful – overcoming.

Looking back, several years after she experienced the Shaman episode, Poet reflects on where her life is now.

> *"I am no longer depressed, for one thing. Nor stressed. My children are grown up and my husband's working part time again. And we've remained married. But only on paper. We live separate lives and have done for many years…I learned a lot about myself and something about men. I have a male friend who I met online about a year ago, but I didn't make the same mistake as with Shaman. I didn't quickly fall in love with him and we've never developed a sexual relationship though there is a lot of affection between us. He is married. His wife has cancer. We've both experienced suffering and we support each other."*

This 'new love' of Poets is helping her recover self-worth and confidence. The relationship is healthy and positive. But Poet has changed. She no longer needs a man in order to feel complete within herself. She has learned self-validation.

"I definitely love myself more than I did. I thought I loved myself as a young woman, but in truth my life had never tested that love. When it got tested, especially in my thirties, I really struggled with depression and low self-esteem. I have had my peaks and troughs, but I've found most benefit from my dress-making, poetry and photography. That has helped me through some very difficult periods."

Faces, thoughts and incidents all recur in the head because the emotion beneath them, and lodged in the heart, needs seeing and processing. Once one can recognise and embrace that emotion in the heart, the mind will be liberated from the persistent noise of recurring thoughts. To clear the mind, one must first engage with the thoughts, look at them deeply and with compassion, see their depth, recognise their origins, and own them. The more one tries to escape the thoughts, the more they will invade the subconscious. There is no escape other than through recognition and positive self-expression. Poet managed to achieve this, though she needed help to do so. That help came via her female friends, her poems, her photography and her dressing-making.

Poet enjoys making those dresses and taking those photos, for two reasons.

1. Her imagination and taste in beauty is superb. She enjoys the power of creating something special for appreciative colleagues and friends. It is the joy of creation and in that process so is she (re)creating herself.

2. She has a very generous and kind soul. She receives vicarious pleasure and satisfaction from other women seeing themselves as beautiful in the dresses and in the photos – which duly get posted on social media, liked, commented upon and received positively.

One of the conditions and consequences of a repetitive memory, the inability to let go of pain and hurt, is fear. Fear feeds on insecurity and insecurity is at the heart of that endless loop, that Groundhog Day of living, whereby we just don't seem able to move on to something new, something better.

Our memory holds us back; it holds us in the grip of fear and insecurity. We have to let it go. We have to become absorbed in the present, not in the past. We must turn our focus to the beauty that already exists in our life, is present and with us every day and every moment.

Poet is no longer fearful. She knows how low she can get, how far down to the bottom life can take her, but she has overcome. Poet has risen to a better place in her life and she has done it in testing circumstances.

Poet still needs validation from other people, but no man can now get the role of sole validator in her life. She is less dependent and therefore much less vulnerable.

Poet has discovered the type of personal validation that really matters – her own.

> *She found herself*
> *wholesome,*
> *and pure*
> *amid*
> *the whirl*
> *of torment*
> *and recklessness.*

Chapter Eleven: Flower

What do you look for in a potential partner? What are your essentials, what are the deal-breakers? We all have our particulars, but If you're a woman searching for a male and you meet a man who is thoughtful, intelligent, sociable, sensitive, never harsh, always considerate, never bullying, always kind, a man who never criticises, is never moody, and has the professional status to help ensure the family has a high-quality material life, then very likely you'd give him at least some consideration. Add in cultural, social, intellectual and sexual compatibility then maybe you'd be tempted to say 'yes' to a relationship, possibly even marriage.

Thirty-one years ago, Flower said 'yes' to such a man. It is a decision she has never regretted.

So why has she spent the past three decades in a state of increasing stress? A stress so severe that it results in insomnia, body rashes and panic attacks? Why is she depressed?

And if she was so in love, why did she embark on a passionate love affair which she fled before she could consummate it?

Clues to this conundrum lie in Flower's authenticity.

Her Authentic Self

Arguably the most important skill humans have is adaptability. We can live in the harshest of climes, overcome the deadliest of diseases, survive the worst terrors, and while all these events are happening around us, to us, still multiply and advance.

But in order to physically thrive, the individual must mentally thrive. And to do that the individual should remain true to itself, its core essence.

What we feel to be who we are, combined with what we believe to be essential truths about the world and about ourselves, creates the self we have to live with.

We are each living with our selves, learning to live with the voice in our heads. Hopefully, learning to love that voice in our heads.

This means that the foremost relationship we ever have in our lives is with our inner self; the entity that whispers to us, which we have incessant discussions with, which occupies a large part of our mind and our heart until we die.

Does this entity have a gender? Very likely. Because it exists at the core of you, within your inner child, then it will inevitably reflect the gender you know you are.

The gender entity of Flower was unquestionably female. She wore beautiful, fashionable dresses; expensive pearls and diamonds adorned her body; the most alluring perfumes enfolded her hands and face.

This was the authentic feminine self that Flower sought to portray to the outside world.

But the inner feminine world of Flower was starving from emotional under-nourishment and the absence of passion.

Her perfect, enviable existence, mirrored in her outwardly ideal marriage, looked amazing on the surface, but inside the family home the woman in Flower was withering away.

Flowers cannot bloom without nourishment. And nor can people. No matter how enchanting the garden, if the individual flower is not sustained then it will die.

For many years, Flower was slowly dying through lack of being able and strong enough to express her authentic feminine self. This true self was parched, weakened and unacknowledged, not least by her. She had denied it for the sake of the marriage.

Why? Because there was no room for femininity in this marriage. Maleness and masculinity overwhelmed it.

The story of Flower is the story of a woman eventually finding and embracing her feminine authenticity, her inner child, through self-love; and duly saving both her self-respect and her relationship.

The Policeman

Flower's early years were peaceful, protective and unexceptional. She came from a middle-class professional, but not wealthy, family. She had ambitions, which were quickly satisfied following her graduation and entry into banking. It is within this domain that she has remained for the past thirty-five years. She is now a branch manager in a quiet suburb of a capital city.

The daily numerical auditing required of a bank manager suits Flower's character. She is highly professional; committed, trustworthy, goal-orientated, hard-working, self-disciplined and rather pedantic. Her life has not been filled with exotic, or indeed, erotic, adventures. She prefers routine to the unknown.

The only adventure Flower has embarked on is marriage and even here she put predictability over passion.

It was in her final year of university that she met the Policeman. A mutual friend's twenty-first birthday party was the moment when Policeman came into her life, where he has remained ever since.

Like Flower, Policeman was also embarking on a life-long career. His graduation from the Police Academy began his career and today he is a Chief Inspector.

The vast majority of recruits into uniformed services such as the police force must undergo physical, mental and emotional transformation, or 'readjustment' in order to fit into the unbending demands of this particular profession. Whatever the country, the police training is almost identical – designed to slot the individual into a hierarchical, totalising, male-dominated, order-based organisation. In other words, the system comes before the individual.

Policeman didn't require moulding. He already was moulded. He was born into a military family and many of his male relations were in the uniformed services. Policeman was raised in a culture where discipline and duty took precedence over individuality and emotional display.

On the outside, and indeed in the minds of both Flower and Policeman, they were a perfect match. Their families knew each other and were friends. They had identical cultural and social values. In fact they had, and still have, so much in common in terms of character-traits that the list is embarrassingly long:

- Dutiful

- Disciplined

- Sensible

- Organised

- Hard working

- Committed

- Goal-orientated

- Pedantic

- Conventional

- Self-controlled

- Loyal

- Self-supporting

- Focused

Of course there were – and still are – some missing elements, essential for any fulfilling relationship, but neither Flower nor Policeman spotted them during their courtship and subsequent marriage at the age of twenty-seven.

Though perhaps a clue could be found in the events leading up to the marriage proposal and in how Policeman proposed to Flower:

> "We courted at first for eight months, and then he told me he had to go abroad for further training. I didn't see him for nearly a year. We had little contact during this time. I thought it was over between us. Other men did ask me out on dates, but none wanted anything serious. Then out of the blue he contacted me again. On the first date after being gone for twelve months he asked me to marry him. He said 'I need a wife and I want to get married'. That was it."

The Marriage

Despite this unromantic proposal, Flower and Policeman didn't exactly approach their marriage like a strategic operation, though from the beginning it was focused and organised.

> "We are a very good team. We work well together and have similar strengths. My husband can be strict if not harsh in his job in the police, but at home he is an ideal partner – supportive, gentle and understanding. We get things done, we cooperate, we establish our goals and work towards them and we are successful as a result."

A great many couples find they can work together as a family unit, and Flower and Policeman were typical of this type of marital arrangement. They started their marriage with a long-term view of what they hoped to achieve together and then set about, as a team, to achieve this. Not surprisingly, their material wealth grew along with their career trajectories.

> "We have invested our disposable income into numerous properties in and outside the city which we rent out."

Flower never felt the need to adjust to her husband's character because she was already familiar with this type of man. Policeman was very much like her father in terms of being reliable and loyal, but also emotionally closed off.

In the thirty years of her marriage, Flower cannot recall a harsh word from her husband. She cannot recall traumatic arguments. But nor can she recall any passion.

> *"I didn't consider passion, or even love, to be the most important aspect for my marriage. I wanted security and predictability. I wanted a husband who would cooperate with me, be my partner, be loyal and trusting."*

Despite the lack of passion in the marriage, it has produced three sons – aged twenty-five, twenty and seventeen.

Flower has the marriage she wanted, though in truth what she has is less a marriage and more a partnership.

The Partnership

As a working-partnership this is a most successful arrangement for Flower and her family. She and her husband work as a team; they overcome difficult and unforeseen circumstances together. They have a no-blame working culture. And they never get into big emotional stand-offs. Their dominant, safest territory is, indeed, the material and the physical, not the emotional. They are strategic and efficient as a working unit. It is this approach that has made them wealthy.

They have, in truth, created an efficient and effective organisational work culture. It is one where the 'strategic priorities' are harmony, union, financial security, ego security, and the physical wellbeing of all, especially the children, all of whom have been educated in expensive private schools.

By contrast, what they regard as the 'small' issues in the family relate to temporary emotional discomfort, personal desire and personal weakness, all the non-physical, non-material aspects of being and belonging.

There is not just a routine and predictability to this partnership, there is a strong expectation of behaviour.

> *"Yes, we have high expectations of each other. But then we know each other and trust that we'll do our duty to the family. Are we perfectionists? I guess we are. Certainly, my husband and I are at work. So it wouldn't be surprising if we carried this over to our*

home life. We don't get side-tracked by emotional stuff. We are too busy with our working lives to let that get in the way of what we have to do."

If this family were to be visited by a team of organisational consultants, it would no doubt be rated very highly on its productivity levels, its efficiency quotient, its profitability, its team work, and its performance indicators. By these standard measurements of work and organisational achievement, the family is impressively successful.

So why is Flower suffering from stress?

The Office

It is a freezing morning in the middle of a northern winter. The night storm has blown itself out and left behind not just snow drifts but also fallen trees and debris-covered roads.

Flower made it into work without a problem, unlike a couple of her staff who are struggling through the commuter traffic. Flower simply judged the likely delay, factored it in, and left home that bit earlier. She is well organised.

Outside temperatures won't get above freezing today, though Flower's office, and the bank branch itself, are warm and comfortable.

But not too warm in Flower's office because it is only 9 a.m. and already she is shivering from anxiety. She has had some breakfast but knows that it is only a matter of time before she has to go to the loo to vomit it up. To staff and customers she appears calm, poised and healthy. But inside her gut is in turmoil. Last night she had just five hours sleep and she'll be taking pills all day to keep her awake and give her energy. She is diagnosed as depressed but functional; a high-functioning depressive. She has deep moods and often lacks motivation to do mundane tasks, but is nevertheless very capable in her work.

> *"I've gone to many doctors but none have been able to tell me what is physically wrong with me. In fact, I don't appear to have any physical ailment. But the anxiety and depression have now been going on for years."*

High-functioning depression is considered an 'invisible illness' in that the people living with it are often high achievers who make you think all is well with them.

> *"It is not like normal depression – it is much harder to treat. But I know there is an underlying cause. I have to hide my condition at*

work and also at home. I have to try and appear in control all the time. It is expected of me by my family and my employers. There are physical symptoms, but I am coming to realise the problem is more psychological than physical."

Flower's office is a place of sanctuary but also a place of potential exposure. She cannot afford to be seen as less than competent, 100% of the time, especially by her staff. Her employers' value her and she is fairly secure in her job, but only as long as she continues to meet the performance criteria. The way she handles this is to double down on commitment, self-discipline and control of her emotions, while maintaining at all times the appearance of high-level managerial and leadership competence. In this regard, Flower is working to her strengths.

Yet the acute anxiety and depression continue.

The Lover

Flower is an intelligent woman. She didn't need a psychiatrist to tell her she was suffering from some form of emotional wellbeing condition. She understood only too well that she wasn't happy, she just didn't know why.

"Actually, I was more than unhappy, I was miserable. My mind was constantly swamped with miserable thoughts. I looked at my luxurious life and couldn't understand how I can be so miserable given all the money I had. Other people I knew with much less seemed to be much happier than myself."

It took an external intervention to push one of her deeply repressed emotions up to the surface. It came in the form of a bunch of roses.

"I'd done a favour for a local businessman, just advised him on a new loan application, and it had gone well for him. He sent me a bunch of roses as a sort of thank you. No one had ever thought to send me flowers before, not even my husband. I was a little shocked, but also happy to receive them."

Flower was even more shocked when that grateful businessman invited Flower to lunch, ostensibly to discuss a business arrangement he needed some banking advice on, but in truth to get to know her better.

Lunch happened and it turned out to be fun for both of them. Within a few weeks she and the businessman were exchanging daily social media messages, compliments, thoughts and, most critically, emotions.

> *"It was the feeling of letting go with my emotional side that had the most impact on me. My marriage was perfect – except it had no passion, no intimacy beyond occasional, routine sex, no feelings were exposed in the family at all. Not by anyone. Everything was controlled, buttoned-down. But then there were no arguments, either. No one got angry or mad at each other. No one said anything nasty to anyone."*

Flower didn't know it but she had moved into an alternative emotional environment, albeit a clandestine one. In this second emotional space she began to explore her feminine senses, including her sexuality.

> *"I had no interest in sex. For me it was a duty to perform. And that was how it was for my husband. As soon as our third son was conceived we pretty much stopped having sex, other than on those occasions when he really wanted to, which wasn't often. But I didn't mind. I never masturbated either. I had just shut myself off, sexually."*

Flower's 'shutting off' wasn't just about sex, it was about her emotional self. This 'affair', yet to be consummated, was stirring up a lot of deep feelings. She realised a disturbing truth, that her marriage was not as good and complete as she'd imagined it to be.

> *"At that point I am really in a quandary. My messages with the businessman were becoming more than just emotional, they had declarations of some very heavy feelings in them. We were also meeting more often and I couldn't continue to make excuses to be seeing him for lunch. But I wanted him. I actually needed this in my life. The passion was glorious. Even though we'd not had sex, to be wanted by this man, desired, just filled me up with joy."*

And yes, while this is passion and joy are increasing, Flower's depression is decreasing.

But is this the answer to Flower's problem? To have an affair?

> *"I was pulled both ways. Frightened, terrified of what I would lose if my husband found out, but filled with glorious joy to be sexually desired as a woman, loved actually."*

Flower held out for as long as she could, about four months, and then agreed to meet her lover-to-be at a business conference in another city. This was intended to be the beginning of their physical relationship.

> *"I got as far as the bedroom with him, but my nerves and anxiety were overwhelming me. I was really sweating badly. I felt physically sick. The idea of undressing and having sex just felt so wrong. Part of me wanted this man, but part of me was repelled at my actions. Then I did a bad thing. I told him I didn't want to be there with him. That is was all my mistake. He was so upset. Really harsh words were said between us. I stormed out in tears. I couldn't speak."*

So traumatised was Flower by her near-miss infidelity, and the emotional backlash it had unleashed, that she couldn't even look at her body in the mirror. She denied it existed. She felt repelled by her nakedness. She didn't wash for six weeks.

The Pain

Flower now has pain in both her heart and in her vagina. She is aching from having dug up and exposed repressed sexual feelings and from having looked into the eyes of a man who wanted her as a woman, but whom she almost immediately rejected.

> *"All this was made worse by another situation in my family. My best friend and her husband. They'd been married for six years but the physical energy and intimacy between them was obvious. I was so envious. They were open about their feelings, candid and natural whereas I felt a fraud as a wife. I felt my marriage was a sham."*

Pain is important. Our bodies need it. Pain is the body's alarm system. And so is emotional distress and depression.

But Flower was actually experiencing more than emotional distress, she was experiencing emotional violence.

And she was inflicting this upon herself.

The Diagnosis

To get towards a diagnosis it is first necessary to consider another aspect of Flower's life; the masculine dominance of her family.

Flower is the only woman in a family of men. And these men all have a common masculine trait: emotional control.

Emotional control in itself is not a bad thing. We all need to control our emotions at times but when it leads to emotional poverty then we have another condition arising: stoicism.

Stoicism is generally understood to mean applying self-control and self-discipline so as to overcome one's emotions, especially those emotions which might be socially judged as negative or destructive or inappropriate. Stoicism is especially common in men and has long informed traditional aspects of masculinity.

But emotions are healthy. All of them are necessary at times in a life, though we shouldn't obsess with negative, damaging emotions like hate and anger. Nevertheless, to try and close down all emotional expression is highly dangerous to the human psyche and limits our ability to recognise, understand and accept our inner self. Emotions are also a release mechanism for a confused and stressed mind.

It is telling that in Flower's family there is no emotional expression – stoicism rules.

All three sons are obsessed with computer games. They spend hours gaming – isolated, not communicating, socially unskilled, emotionally dysfunctional,and utterly uninterested in the world beyond the screen.

> *"My eldest son is severely dysfunctional, socially. He is what is called 'hikikomori' which is a Japanese term and means he suffers from acute social withdrawal. He dropped out of university and is now effectively a recluse at home. He just stays in his bedroom and plays on his computer. I just hope my other two sons aren't like this"*

Some aspects of stoicism and emotional poverty and which are present in Flower's family:

1. They are very goal-orientated and competitive. They are also organised and highly functional. They have a long-term view and a clear order or priority in their life.

2. Minute and excessive attention is given to external manageable situations: Flower obsesses over her work; Policeman obsesses over his career; the three sons obsess over gaming. There is an overarching obsession with money and wealth accumulation. This is a mental deflection arising from fear of what is deep inside them.

3. There is overall very poor awareness of their own emotions. Emotions are either unseen or treated as external noise/ emotional disturbance or totally denied.

4. They are afraid to touch their inner selves, their inner thoughts that stem from desires, fears, resentment and other emotions.

They wrongfully believe that the only way to satisfy their inner self is to satisfy it in physical and material manners. They are not aware of a powerful alternative which is to embrace all emotions and thoughts with tolerance, appreciation and (most importantly) love.

5. They are fearful of losing control, which for them means acting in any way which might be consider improper, risky, adventurous, different or emotive. They avoid voicing their inner needs for fear of causing problems, discomfort, disdain or negative judgement in each other. This fear leads to their failure to express their emotions in a positive, healthy way.

6. They imagine they take good care of each other and contribute to the wellbeing of the home by being stoic. In truth, they are denying the core identity of each other and starving the home and family of emotional sustenance and individual expression.

7. Positive feelings and emotions like fun, excitement, joy, fulfilment and passion are absent in daily life. They are in emotional poverty, despite their material luxury and abundance.

8. Because they can never risk abandoning their impassivity and dispassion they cannot liberate their inner selves – they cannot experience pure euphoria and delight.

Finally, we may try to repress emotions so they are not seen on the surface, though not confronting these feelings in ourselves doesn't mean they disappear. They don't magically go away. They arise in our body. The three males in the family can feel secure in their masculine identity by appearing stoic simply because excessive emotional control is (still) a culturally accepted way of being a man. Indeed, for Policeman, being stoic is actually considered an advantage in his career where emotional expression is deemed threatening to leadership and a rule-based order. But this is not the case for Flower, a woman and a feminine being. Flower has spent over thirty years trying to deny her emotional self which in effect means denying who she really is.

Toxic Stoic Femininity

The toxic femininity that Flower experiences is partly a condition of her husband's masculine character, but also of the male-dominated culture which has developed in the home since they were married. That is not to blame either him nor her for this situation; both Flower and her husband have jointly created this family culture, this world where inner feelings are repressed, emotions are denied and true selves aren't permitted to surface.

The warning signs were apparent from the start of the relationship, especially the way in which Policeman approached the proposal. He did not express any emotional joy and desire to Flower before they got married and he certainly hasn't done so since. There was no passion back then, and their marriage has been devoid of it ever since. But Flower accepted that proposal and therefore accepted the man behind it. She must have had her reasons. But was love one of them? Or more importantly, does he love her today, does she love him?

> "I think he loves me. He never tells me. But then I never tell him I love him, either. It just gets assumed. We are not a tactile family. We don't go in for loving hugs and all that stuff. We don't forget birthdays but neither do we have parties and big fun times. The way the family operates is that everyone has their own room, we are each on a computer doing our own thing, and we live in this compartmentalised way. I think a lot of families are like this nowadays. Are we any different? I don't think so. But maybe we are a little extreme."

Flower and Policeman have placed prosperity and the 'smooth' running of the family as priorities over emotional expression and loving passion and have done so for over thirty years. Family members do not demonstrate affection with each other: they never have.

And as the three sons get older, this type of masculine culture is becoming more entrenched with each member focused only on their own activities, not on each other.

Communication between them is stilted and sterile, limited to small talk only. No one makes emotional waves. Nothing important gets said, unless it is regards material, physical aspects of life. Her eldest son has absorbed all this and has now totally withdrawn from society.

The result, at least for Flower, is depression, sleepless nights and anxiety.

She is not in touch with her inner femininity. It is denied, rendered if not problematic then at least invisible. This is the toxic femininity manifest in her life and in her body.

All these physical conditions are present in Flower and none can be resolved by medicine, pills or visits to the hospital. They are evidence of the emotional violence given to her inner self manifesting into her physical self.

The Remedy

The basic approach to addressing the vacuum in Flower's life (and indeed in the whole family) is straightforward, though it is rarely undertaken without external guidance because first the family must recognise the problem before they can approach a solution. So long as they are fixated on material and physical dimensions of life, and remain ignorant of their need for self-appreciation, then no progress will be made.

But, in short, the key is to connect with their emotions and develop self-awareness.

1. Learn to name their emotions (like loneliness, low self-esteem, self-doubt) and link them to negative thoughts in their brain (e.g. this problem is too big for me to handle! I am not attractive any more! I am a failure!) and physical conditions in their body (such as insomnia, anxiety, depression and feeling cold).

2. Learn to link their emotional, physical states to the external circumstances (e.g. lack of passion and appreciation in a marriage).

3. Learn to name and embrace their needs and wishes (e.g. the desire to be seen, understood and protected).

4. Learn to negotiate and balance themselves when conflicting needs simultaneously exist. (e.g. the need to submit/contribute to the wholeness of the family versus their inner need to be emotionally free: the need to be externally strong versus the need to be authentically vulnerable and dependent).

All of this comes down to self-love combined with self-management and to achieve this healthy state Flower and her family should practise the following:

1. Learn to recognise, respect and tolerate all their emotions, needs and desires.

2. Accept that all emotions are important and should be treated with care and appreciation.

3. Learn to appreciate and love themselves unconditionally (be their best friend)

4. Learn not to sacrifice themselves for the purpose of pleasing others.

5. Learn to tolerate themselves for disliking, rejecting or loathing certain people and things.

6. Learn to give sovereignty to themselves.

Basically, being stoic is not bad, nor is emotional control. But it becomes toxic when it dominates a family, a work culture, or indeed a person – when it serves to obliterate the full character of an individual for the sake of social and cultural appearances.

When that happens, the persistent self-denial – combined with failure to love who one truly is – results in a warped personality; someone who is good at maintaining social appearances but fails to know who they really are. At that point, self-love is impossible.

Where Is She Now?

Following the failed love affair and continuing mental wellbeing problems, Flower plumbed the depths of self-recrimination, guilt and disrespect. As she put it:

> *"I came to feel sorry for my husband. My sex with him is not good, my housekeeping is bad, even my cooking is poor. I am overweight. I am not attractive. Why is he with me, I thought."*

But this period marked the turning point in her life…

> *"Right at the time I was feeling the lowest, I met a long-time friend of mine who had gone through something similar to me. She spoke to me about self-love and about forgiving myself. She gave me some practices to do and this started me on the road to recovery."*

The practices that Flower now follows are very simple:

1. Start by looking in the mirror and talking to yourself, saying loving, nurturing words, give yourself loads of positive strokes but also don't hold back from recognising where you went wrong.

2. Forgive yourself from being wrong, bad and improper; promise and trust that you will learn from the mistakes and become a better version of yourself every new day.

3. Put your hand across your chest, over your heart, and feel the emotion of the moment. Allow it to flow through you and welcome it. Don't resist it. Whether it be pain, fear, joy, passion or love, accept it is within you and listen to it.

4. Allow what is in you to emerge and embrace it with tender attention, marvel at its power and duration. Allow the emotion to be itself, the way a mother would love her only child unconditionally.

5. Talk with yourself more often. Say kind words. Play games with yourself. Laugh with yourself. Don't pretend your inner self, your inner child, doesn't exist. Embrace it.

Whenever possible, Flower combines these practices with meditation, though she doesn't claim to be an expert on this:

"For me, meditation is simply being quiet, sitting or lying still, finding time to be within myself without external interruptions. I can do it in my office at work, during lunch hour; I can do it for five minutes before I go to bed; I can do it early in a morning, just after I wake up."

The result has been remarkable. Flower is fast transforming herself and her life. In her first-ever self-talk, flower enjoyed currents of exceptional warmth and excitement running through her back and loins. And after each self-talk she noticed her anxiety and depression reduced significantly. Each self-talk developed its own direction and speed, leaving Flower amazed by her own intelligence and strength. She is anew each new day and very quickly her husband could see a transformation.

"Even my husband noticed the difference. We talked about what was troubling me and he seemed to understand. We have had some really heartfelt conversations. We have renewed our interest in each other and the marriage is stronger for that. We are now closer. He has long had problems with sleeping and it is getting better for him too. So we're both on a new path."

Flower is in the process of creating intimacy with herself, loving herself outside of social conventions and expectations. But first she needed to recognise what she had become and this didn't happen until she'd suffered substantial emotional violence to her body and mind.

"A new door has opened within me and to enter it I've had to dis-identify with the woman I'd become, especially the wife I had become. That wasn't easy and I was scared at first. But my mental wellbeing was so damaged, my self-respect so reduced, that I had no choice. I had to do something."

This change in Flower's life has been going on now for just a year, so it is too early to say where she'll be in the years ahead. But she is most definitely curving upwards.

Flower now begins each day with anticipation and wonder, because she won't know what excitement her self-talk with bring about. She ends each day with gratitude for what she has and pride in her striving towards self-development.

She has reached down and lifted up her authentic feminine self from the cold depths. It was withered but now it is getting nourished. She has learned so many hard lessons and is still learning them. She still needs to learn to put herself first, not always her family. She still needs to talk to her sons openly but also critically when necessary. She needs to develop the new dialogue with her husband and share with him her feelings, while encouraging him to share his. She needs to focus less on duty and more on self-care.

There was a period in Flower's life when she stopped breathing life into her soul. She imagined she was alive but the life she had was no real life at all. She had duty but no sense of duty of care to herself. She had management but no self-management. And she had intelligence but no emotional self-awareness.

The lesson from Flower's story is that appearances do not count so much as what is going on below the surface, what is in a person's heart. If self-love is not present then that cannot be compensated for by career, houses or wealth. When self-love is absent then so will the body express this lack through physical ailments. When a person is not able to be their authentic self then don't expect wellness to be present.

The second lesson is that families that allow traditional masculinity to dominate will suffer from emotional dysfunctionality. They may well appear successful and accomplished to outsiders, but the family essence is toxic and damaging to all who connect with it. These are not families but political arrangements, pragmatic conveniences.

Flower's marriage will survive. It deserves to. And so too will Flower. The changes occurring now are powerful and fast; there is colour in her face and in her life. She is finally blooming.

> *"I love flowers but never bought them. Now I have bowls of flowers all over the house, and in my office. I discovered joy in these little things. I'm rediscovering life."*

Look into your eyes in the mirror,
my lady.

You will see
sorrows
insecurities
fears
shame
angers
hurts
pains
...

You can soak them all
in the ocean of Love
in your own heart.

You can warm them up
in the flames of Love
in your own eyes.

You can lullaby them all
with your songs of Love
until they all fall asleep.

You can caress them
till they bloom into Love flowers
in your soul garden.

You
have
the magic!

Because
deep down your core,
you
are
Love.

Chapter Twelve: Bird

Flying Ever Higher, Flying Solo

Is marriage an opportunity or is it a trap? For many couples, it is both. We may start out in love, but then we imagine the only way to 'secure' such love is to legalise it. At which point we learn one of life's more important lessons: that love and the law don't mix. The former is informed by the heart, the latter by a judicial system.

But a marriage need not become a trap if the two individuals in it stick to one vital, immutable rule: *never change.*

Of course, there is not much chance of that happening. We change constantly in minor ways we barely notice and occasionally in big ways we cannot help but notice.

What then becomes of the two lovers, now wife and husband? They have each changed over the years, they are each somewhat different and so are their feelings for each other. Yet the marriage remains, fixed in a judicial system which will judge them and penalise them, perhaps harshly, for having 'failed'.

The love that blossomed so magnificently has become at its worst hate, at its best disappointment and likely costly – materially and emotionally – to both former lovers.

Who is to blame? It depends on the marriage, but often it is no single individual. Rather we should cast a critical eye on unrealistic expectations.

But what is love if not a heady interlude of unrealistic expectations experienced in an otherwise mundane and predictable life? Maybe we are entitled to have, indeed need to have, unrealistic expectations now and again.

Humans are nourished by love, validated by love, emboldened by love, comforted by love, but mostly given hope by love. And yet this essential, almost compulsive element of the human condition remains indefinable and amorphous.

This brings us back to the known and the predictable – which is that every human being undergoes change during their lifetime, though some of us change more slowly than others.

A marriage born out of love and passion, inhabited by two individuals, one of whom barely changes at all but the other who changes so fast she is now flying higher and higher, like the bird on the wind, leaving her mate behind. This is her story.

The Nest

The marriage which birthed the life of Bird was a good one. It still is. Her mum and dad remain not just married but in love, though they've had their problems, notably her mum's persistently poor health. The couple don't consider their relative poverty to be a problem – no one in their community is wealthy. And anyway, dad has a solid, life-long job in local government. They count their blessings. And well they might, not least because they've produced four healthy, happy children.

As in any nest of chicks, one will likely stand out as the strongest, the brightest, the chick most likely to flourish and prosper – Bird.

Nurtured by her loving and supportive family, Bird grew fast. At the age of eighteen she left the family home for university, where she trained to be a teacher. Her siblings remained in the nest. Bird was eager to learn not just how to teach but about life. She read books, reflected and began to observe the wider world around her. She grew knowledgeable and confident.

Did the growing Bird have high hopes and expectations? Yes, but they were tempered by a powerful and pervasive condition existing within the family nest; gender expectations. Her mum never had a full-time job, only occasional part-time work. Her dad was the family breadwinner, a kind and generous man who understood his role very clearly – to be the provider for his family.

Bird assimilated these gender values and their associated roles. The message they gave out, often overtly reinforced by mum and dad, was very clear; get a husband, become a wife and start your own family. Place every other hope and expectation secondary to these rules.

This dominant discourse was already firmly assimilated into Bird's mind after she graduated and started looking for her first teaching post.

This was the toxic femininity that Bird would one day have to unshackle herself from it she was ever to fly high.

Flying Solo

It didn't take long for Bird to find that job. Within a few weeks she was offered a teaching position in a prestigious, family-owned private school in the city. She was twenty-two and living an independent life as a fully-fledged professional, far away from the family home both physically and emotionally. She had stepped out the nest and begun her first flight. Not too far away but far enough for her to miss the safety and comfort of the nest.

Flying solo was fun, exciting and rewarding. But she often felt lonely in that big, anonymous city.

Bird ameliorated that loneliness through immersing herself in stories, in books, in the world of the narrative. She spent hours in romantic novels, in compelling adventure stories and in the biographies of the famous. Looking back, she realises there was a clear indicator in her choice of books as to where her life was heading.

> *"I love to read both fiction and non-fiction, but when I look back on the types of books I used to read in my twenties, I can see a clear pattern. There was invariably a heroine, shaking off convention and hardship in order to pursue her dreams. Sometimes she had a lover, sometimes not, or she might have many lovers, but she was always her own woman."*

Bird was not yet her own woman. She may have imagined being so, but that dream of the independent, free-flying Bird had yet to confront the dominant discourse of gender identity and fixed binary roles.

At this point in her life, ready to fly ever upward propelled by ambition, aspiration and determination, Bird could have begun to realise her dream. Instead, she chose safety and security – with the added ingredient of passion. All this was packaged in a man she chanced to meet when she returned to the family home for a weekend visit.

He was the same age as Bird, good-looking and from her home town. He was of her family's background: working class, provincial but uneducated and unambitious. The relationship started tentatively enough, mostly online. But very quickly the feelings developed. Within weeks he was professing his love for Bird.

They dated for four years, and then got married at the age of twenty-eight.

Bird didn't realise it then, but she has actually made a life-transforming choice which she fervently believed was made in her heart but was in reality made in her brain.

> *"My husband was the perfect choice for me back then. I was fed up living alone. My teaching job was going well but I needed someone in my life. I was lonely. He was very similar to my father; steady and*

reliable, plus he came from the same social class, the same cultural background as my family. Maybe I felt I was maintaining a link with that background by marrying him. And he was passionate. Our intimate life was very good and that brought pleasure into my life. The sort of pleasure you cannot find in books."

Unconditional romantic love is the rarest of all loves. And Bird hadn't found it. What she had found, rooted out, was the much more common type of love – conditional. The type requires that the one we could love must first tick a number of boxes before we fall.

The boxes which Bird's husband ticked were fairly clear; familiar cultural background, appropriate social class, the right age, traditionally masculine and sexually passionate. In other words, safe and familiar.

Bird was flying solo but she was lonely. Having a husband would solve that problem.

Bird was passionate and she needed physical intimacy in her life. Having a husband would solve that problem.

Bird hated coming home to an empty apartment. Another lifestyle problem resolved by her husband.

Bird loved her job but she never truly felt she belonged in the city. With a husband beside her she no longer had to feel anxious about not belonging. She had her own family to belong to.

But mostly Bird loved the way this man loved her. He was persistent, and that was the single quality that most melted her heart. He pursued Bird for four years while they dated at a distance. He never gave up.

Unfortunately, Bird didn't realise her choice of husband came with a condition attached. The condition was that she would have to change to accommodate him.

Accommodating Toxic Femininity

With some women, toxic femininity thrusts itself upon them and stabs them in the heart. In others, it slowly creeps up like a noxious cloud; enveloping them, suffocating out life and hope. Many millions more are born into this culture and can never find the strength or opportunity to challenge it. Then there are those, like Bird, who choose toxic femininity.

"By the time I left university I was a free-thinking, independent woman. I didn't buy into all the gender conventions which my family lived by. But my husband had no such thinking. He was, still is, a traditional type of guy. He and I couldn't talk about gender roles

and identity. He just wouldn't understand it. He has no language for this level of discussion. But I wanted our marriage to succeed so I knew I would have to accommodate his reality rather than he try and accommodate mine. So I changed myself to be more traditional. I played the role of dutiful wife. I kept quiet about my professional life, my ambitions. I let him play the role of dominant male in the relationship. I deliberately played the minor role in the marriage to make him feel good about himself. I knew I was doing this but I felt it necessary. Of course, I was mistaken."

This gender play-acting went on for five years. During that time, and against her better judgement, Bird played the role as well as she was able. Bird acquiesced when her husband said he wanted to open a small shop and used up their meagre savings to do so. The business failed. She supported him when he quit his full-time retail job to take up as an insurance salesman, promised high commission. He failed to get paid any commission. And she helped him fill in the college application for a diploma in travel and tourism. He quit after three months. She appreciated her husband trying to improve himself, to be the family breadwinner, but sadly she came to realise he lacked the skills and resilience to do so. As far as being the male family breadwinner, it was, and still is, Bird.

But there was an additional factor now emerging in this increasingly complex marriage: infertility.

One of the factors drawing Bird to marriage was the prospect of having children. In that regard, she and her husband were of the same mind. Unfortunately, while the sex was great and the physical passion very evident, conception never followed. After four years of trying, they tried IVF treatment. Twice. This didn't work either.

It was fortunate that Bird was now heading upwards in her teaching career and able to benefit from a higher salary, because not least due to the IVF treatments, the family finances were being stretched tight.

What was also being stretched tight, sometimes to breaking point, was her marriage.

"No, I wasn't happy in the marriage. I was becoming a different person. I was always angry, always frustrated and always unhappy. Sex with my husband didn't alleviate all that. When I was newly married I thought it would be easy to be the quiet, traditional wife, doing the conventional things married women are expected to do, behave like the dutiful, obedient wife. But then I realised I was trapped. I had demeaned myself, for what?

Bird had imagined that compromising her life, who she was, in order to secure her marriage – in effect accommodating toxic femininity – could be managed and could be controlled. But she was young and naïve. Toxic femininity came to invade her sense of self. Her self-love diminished. She was still a woman but not a woman she now respected. She was angry, sure, but mostly with herself. She was most definitely frustrated but with how she had let herself down. And inevitably she was unhappy.

The bird had started out with great hopes and the ability to soar high, but instead had caged itself.

Would Bird have felt differently had she become pregnant? Maybe. At least for a few years. But with women like Bird there is an inevitability to their ambition. Driven by deep-rooted frustration and a growing awareness that life does not need to be lived in the shadow of the man, this ambition will surface sooner or later. And when it does, all the years of play-acting as the dutiful, pliant, passive wife will erupt in an unbridled outpouring of recrimination.

At that point, many husbands will simply stand back in amazement – utterly bewildered at what they perceive as an unreasonable, over-emotional, if not wilful change in their previously docile wife. What did I do wrong, they will demand? Have I not loved you, they will beg? What can I do to make it better, they will plead? What more do you want from me, they will accuse?

Bird is not the type of woman to get into emotional histrionics. She is quiet but focused. Her husband never had any idea all this turmoil was occurring in her mind. She protected him from it – another example of the lingering effects of toxic femininity, you might say.

What she did instead, was take to the wing.

Taking Off

The second failed IVF treatment sealed it for Bird. While she continued to outwardly agree with her husband's desire for a child, she took her future into her own hands. She began a part-time MA in Education.

The cost was not a problem as this was partly born by her school. Bird had the spare time to devote to the study and so she simply settled into a new routine of more reading and writing.

Doing a first degree can, nowadays, almost feel like a rite of passage for many students, whether male or female. It is an expectation fuelled by the fact that so many young people now go to university. It is a normalised ambition, certainly among the middle classes. But postgraduate programmes are rather different. They require a higher level of commitment not least because they are undertaken during the income-generating years. Maybe this is one of the reasons why postgraduate degrees can be such life-changing events in people's lives. To suddenly have to accommodate higher-level study, while also working full-time, impacts on a person's sense of who they are and what they might become. It raises the bar.

Such was the situation with Bird. By the time she finished the MA, two years later, she was a changed woman.

> "I did the MA in order to advance my career as a teacher. I planned to stay at the school and just progress up the management ladder. I was already a Head of Department. But something else happened during that time which I had not anticipated. I became more independent. I started thinking more critically about my life and the direction it was going in. For me, the MA was a period of academic success and personal advancement. I grew in confidence and this impacted on my marriage."

With a BA an MA, and now promoted to Head of Department, Bird could no longer continue to accept the additional identity of housekeeper. She grew resentful of her husband's unwillingness to adapt practically and emotionally to her new, empowered female identity. Or maybe, she reflected, he just doesn't see this new me? Am I that invisible to him, she asked herself? If so, who does he imagine I am, or more importantly, who does he imagine he loves?

These key questions never got answered because they never got asked. Both Bird and her husband remained silent as to what was actually happening in their marriage, in their relationship.

He no doubt imagined that his life with Bird would carry on as 'normal' and into the future, with the only possible change being the additional of an, as yet to be conceived, child. His role as the perceived man of the house would remain, only to be emboldened as a father. But what about Bird? Where did she now fit into this traditional gender family set-up?

The inability or unwillingness of Bird and her husband to identify, examine and mutually explore the fundamental shift in their relationship, meant that silence became a killer. The marriage continued, the sex continued, but intellectually, professionally and personally Bird was now flying higher and higher. All the while her husband remained behind in an increasingly cold and empty nest.

"Of course, he sensed something was amiss but he couldn't put it into words. Or he chose not to. Instead he became sulky, moody. When we had arguments, mostly about doing the housework, shopping, and stuff like that, it came out about how he felt inferior to me. He was unhappy and miserable. I know he felt emasculated by my success but how could I discuss that with him? He didn't understand the concepts involved. Whenever we got close to talking about roles he retreated to the thinking he'd been brought up with – that the man of the house is the boss and the woman's role is to support him. For me this was now just ridiculous. I had changed, a lot. He hadn't changed at all."

Despite the professional advancement that Bird had enjoyed so far, she remained at heart a provincial woman. She had achieved far beyond her family's expectations and indeed her own original ambitions, but she was unsure as to how much further she might travel.

She saw no new horizons. She was aiming only to remain at the school until retirement, many years hence.

Bird and her husband continued to try for a child, but by now it had become a predictable, routine matter. If conception followed, fine, if not, that was fine too. At least this approach reduced the tension between them. They settled into an accommodation. Bird had completed her MA, her husband had a full-time job, their finances were improving, and they had only themselves to consider. No baby was on the horizon. Arguments about roles and responsibilities reduced though the underlying issues remained.

But this routine was about to be disturbed. A new horizon was beckoning and it was made visible by an entirely unexpected source.

A New Horizon Beckons

It was late spring when the educational management consultant, an experienced academic, appeared at the school to undertake advisory work for the school owners. He duly made it is job to talk to all the key employees, especially the Heads of Department. It was during such a meeting with Bird that she took the opportunity to tell him about her current research at the school. Bird had enjoyed the MA so much she had decided to continue doing more research, possibly getting it published in an academic journal. She presented her work to the consultant, wondering if he might advise her on how to improve it.

The outcome was not what Bird had expected.

> *"He took the writing and research away and read it. Then he came back to me with suggestions for improvement. But the most staggering suggestion he made was that I should now consider doing a doctorate, a PhD in Education. He said that while the research was ongoing and the article was not yet ready for submission to a journal, the quality of the writing and the research indicated PhD level ability. I was so delighted. I never told my husband but from that moment on, I knew where I was heading."*

Sometimes all it takes is a single vote of confidence to set someone on an entirely new or higher path. Bird was already flying high but the professional assessment of someone she knew and respected drove her to new heights. She now saw an entirely new horizon beckon: herself as a Doctor of Education.

Where Is She Now?

Following the surprising but most welcome comments from the consultant, Bird acted with fierce resolve. She researched where she might undertake a PhD, both with and without a scholarship. The two favoured countries which emerged were New Zealand and Australia.

At time of writing, she is in contact with a prestigious university in New Zealand and has begun producing her draft doctorate proposal and letter of application.

She is clear as to what she wants to research.

She is clear as to where she wants to research it.

She is clear as to how to fund the research.

What she is not clear about is whether or not to take her husband with her.

Bird is well aware that this is the big moment in her life. Everything else she has experienced can be seen as a prelude to what happens next, very likely as a doctoral candidate in a New Zealand university. She cannot know where she will be at the end of this study, probably in four years' time. She may never return to her home country to live, or she might. She is unlikely to return to her current school.

Still aged only thirty-four, the horizon she sees is as wide as her imagination. The possibilities are both inspiring and intimidating.

Bird is intelligent and reflective. She knows herself and she knows her weaknesses.

"I have a tendency to feel isolated, lonely. I can easily feel like an outsider, like I don't belong. This happened when I first moved to the city and my new job. Is it going to happen again when I go to New Zealand? Possibly. In which case, having my husband with me will help me feel less lonely, help me settle in. Despite our problems he is not a bad husband. He loves me, he is honest and he is faithful. I enjoy our physical relationship but he is not my equal, intellectually. We are more like brother and sister. That is the way our marriage is heading."

The love that existed at the start of the marriage has mostly disappeared, to be replaced by an accommodation, at least on Bird's part. All the narrative of attachment that Bird engages in reinforces the truth, which is that she loves being loved by her husband but doesn't love him back.

She has begun to unhook the emotional connection and has started the process of letting go. Inevitably, this will eventually result in him meaning nothing to her, or not enough to continue a life with him.

There are still hooks which hold her back. There is the physical side of their relationship. Bird is a passionate woman and her husband continues to satisfy that need. She is not the type to start hunting for a new mate in a new country.

But the biggest hook is Bird's continuing attachment not to her husband but to toxic femininity. She is not totally done with the idea that a woman is better with a husband than without one. She still views single women (spinsters) and divorcees with pity.

"Being single again seems so high a price to pay. I look at women who are single, divorced, and I don't want to be like them. I want a husband and I already have one. I just want a husband who can accept the new me."

Aligned with Bird's increasingly assertive and self-confident self, there exists a soft, traditionally feminine, dependent woman. In other words, Bird has her own masculine/feminine identity mix, a gender dichotomy with tensions and contradictions, but which nevertheless holds her to her husband and holds her together as a woman.

But can this gender dualism, this identity mix of Bird's, survive the doctorate?

If Bird takes her husband to New Zealand, then the consequence will be a continuation of the compromise of self which she first accepted at the start of her marriage. Toxic femininity will be diminished, for sure, but not fully eradicated. She will still be lacking the depth of self-love needed to fly to her furthest heights. She will attempt to fly high while carrying with her a moody, frustrated, increasingly bewildered husband.

If Bird does not take her husband to New Zealand, then she has two issues to face.

1. Recognising her propensity for isolation and non-belonging, she must find the depth of self-love to overcome this; the inner self-sufficiency to belong only to her self not to an idealised model of traditional wife.

2. She has to resolve the dilemma of how to let go of him.

The one question she must ask herself – and answer very soon is this:

> "I know what the question is. Am I going to leave my husband eventually anyway? If so, then best to do it now, in his home country, where he's close to his family. To do it in a year or so's time, when he's in New Zealand would be doubly cruel."

Without Distortion

The Bird that flew the family nest nearly twenty years ago is rather different to the Bird about to fly off to the other side of the world in pursuit of a PhD. She has been changed by events but she has also changed herself. Bird has much greater self-knowledge, self-sufficiency and self-confidence. She has recognised how trying to be a compliant wife harmed her and she's forgiven herself for that mistake. She is still learning to live for herself but remains needy as a woman. Her mindset remains somewhat influenced by the toxic elements and restrictions contained in traditional feminine identity. In that respect, Bird has yet to get over her upbringing. Certainly, doing a doctorate in education is going to impact Bird massively, though quite how massively she cannot yet know. But for sure she will be a different Bird at the end of it.

But perhaps the biggest change in Bird is that she has learned to see herself, and her husband, without distortion. She has removed most of the gender blinkers that previously stopped her understanding herself as a woman, and him as a man. Some blinkers remain, but the doctorate will very likely see them come off. And when that happens she will be faced with the reality of having lived her life under a gender discourse which served to inhibit her propensity for self-actualisation. Will she feel bitter? Only if she has regrets.

De-Programming

Central to Birds' story so far is the issue of identity accommodation, which in her case emerges through her willingness to compromise her life for the sake of her marriage. This is a compromise between her social-professional development for the sake of or sense of belonging. But Bird is not alone in making such a compromise. Throughout history, women have been programmed to rely on a man, to find shelter in a male heart, and to create cosiness in some kitchen, under some roof. It has been instilled in them throughout the timeline of human civilization. That weakness, softness and neediness effectively controls women's choices. It influences their sense of what it means to be a complete woman. They come to enjoy being weak, dependent and needy.

Yet often they fail to recognise that the person they choose to rely on is, in fact, so weak, unstable, empty and unfunctional as to be no support to them whatsoever. This man they choose to rely on, to protect them, often is completely incapable of providing such support. When the woman realises this truth, frustrations and conflicts arise. The woman may try to 'help' that man to be a man, but usually they fail. The man cannot be man enough for them.

At that point, three options emerge and each is open to Bird:

1. Get rid of that man and look for another man who is masculine enough for them. In this case, they are brave enough to let go of an emotional connection, but they stay programmed to the gender ideology which trapped them in the first place. If Bird takes this route she will have developed courage and some self-love, but remain hooked to the notion of woman in need of a man in order to be complete, in which case she risks remaining as the 'other' in the relationship and in her own self-perception. But at least she will have the chance to thrive, not merely survive.

2. Get rid of that man, and go solo; learn to find shelter in their own heart, *be their own woman,* be self-sufficient. Women like Bird have a lot of inner strength, more than they are aware of. She will unlearn/ deprogram the need for a shelter in a male heart, and learn that she can be quite enough for herself. She can even go further: learn to love herself and protect herself on behalf of the "ideal" man that she may meet in the future. While unlearning and deprogramming, she also creates a new identity – she is a human being capable of flying solo, she is a

woman with self-reliance. If Bird takes this route she will learn to embrace her loneliness and transform it into strength for self-development.

3. Stay with that man and simultaneously deprogram herself, creating their new identity, becoming self-sufficient and empowering herself. During that process, they can also help the man to deprogram himself, re-invent himself, and evolve upward into a better male version of himself. Then both of them will have their new relationship identity and new connection and can fly up together. This can be done if the woman has compassion, empathy and care for the man, and the patience, willingness and skill to be the man's guide. The woman will learn to give a lot to the man while giving a lot to herself. United, they develop their compassion, tolerance and wisdom in unison. But this option requires the man to be capable and willing of such a transformation. If Bird takes this route she needs to be fairly confident her husband can play his part, not merely be a bystander in Bird's solo flight to the stars.

Which option is Bird likely to choose? She is surely not taking the first choice. She is re-programming herself and developing fast. Her temporary weakness (staying with her husband) might be an indicator that she has the potential to reach option three at some future point of time if her husband also has the inner strength to become a new man. But failing that happening, and fairly soon, then option two looks most likely.

What Kind of Bird?

Flight is a gift given to birds and it is a beautiful sight to see them soar to the heavens, apparently unencumbered by gravity. There is a freedom in the flight of birds that humans can only envy. But humans can fly metaphorically. They can soar to the outer limits of their imagination, hopes, abilities and ambitions. Such a human is Bird. She is remarkable in some ways but unremarkable in others. There will be many women reading her story who see themselves portrayed within it. Bird's story is compelling precisely because it touches the very issues at the heart of contemporary femininity and masculinity; the choices available to women to pursue their own lives unencumbered by the gravity pull of traditional gender ideology and patriarchal values. Bird is all women.

But what type of bird is she?

Well, Bird is brave. She has the heart of a fierce fighter. She is on the journey of rejecting the limits placed upon her by her family, society and herself, and reinventing her capabilities and possibilities. She now sees far into the distance. She will soon be unstoppable.

Bird is an eagle. If you are fortunate you may see it one day soaring above you, courageous, independent, alone and majestic in the heavens. The queen of birds.

In your depth
lies
the magic sword
that can slash
all the knots
in
the quandaries
of
your soul.

Hold it,
and
chop
them all up!
My sweet girl,
you are
also
a
fierce fighter!

133

3: The Self-Loving Women

Chapter Thirteen: Alchemist

TURNING TRAUMA INTO BEAUTY

To live as a woman is to live with feelings but also with vulnerability – to be endlessly exposed to the emotional forces sweeping around you. As a result, no woman can live a life without experiencing pain. It is a condition of the gender. A woman might try and harden her heart to the possibilities of pain and heartbreak, protect herself in various ways – not least through toxic femininity – but there is no complete and sure immunity. Pain will pierce the hardest of feminine hearts.

So how to survive as a woman? How to thrive as a woman in a world which still treats you as the second sex, the weaker gender, the follower not the leader, the object not the subject? A world where suffering is guaranteed?

The emotional depths within women are beyond the comprehension of most men, though men can sense it, which is why they try to control it. When a woman does cast off her emotional inhibitions, duly exposing her raw female self, she is awesome and fearsome. Men do tremble when the Goddess arises.

Every woman has a Goddess inside her but not every woman lets her rise. Many accept the conditions imposed upon them by a gender order not of their making and not designed for their benefit. Many cooperate in their own submission. Many are complicit in the submission of other women.

But not every woman. As we show in this book, increasing numbers are rising and declaring their inner Goddess not least to themselves.

Such a woman is Alchemist. Why is she an alchemist? Because she has turned her pain into possibility, into agency, and into an independent womanhood. She has learned to treasure suffering and embrace it, because when she does she grows stronger.

Impoverishment

Poverty might be relative but impoverishment certainly is not. To be impoverished means to literally have nothing. Not enough shelter, not enough food, not enough of the essentials necessary to keep life and body functioning. Alchemist was impoverished. She slept in a single room apartment with her siblings and parents. She walked miles to school each day and in all weathers. She relied on school dinners for nourishment. She had no clothes of her own, only castoffs from other families. She did not even have any underwear. When she had her first period the blood trickled down her leg, to the shock and amusement of her school friends. But she was at least fortunate to be at school. Her father wanted her to quit school at the age of thirteen and start work, to help contribute to the family's income, which was a pittance anyway.

But then teachers and neighbours stepped in and donated money so that Alchemist could continue her education.

Why? Because by then Alchemist, despite being impoverished, was demonstrating some of the intelligence and resolve which would enable her to eventually carve out a successful life. Despite this life of pauperism, somewhere and somehow Alchemist had acquired a brain and her teachers spotted it.

The childhood of Alchemist was lacking not just material quality, it was lacking emotional and intellectual quality.

> *"We had no books at home, nothing to read, and there were always tensions in the family. All of us having to live in a single room apartment put pressure on everyone. My father would disappear for days at a time, sometimes weeks, and then come back with some money for my mother. She raised us three children but she aged fast and her health was very poor."*

When Alchemist was fourteen, her father died in a road accident. This left the family even worse off than before. Her mother quickly remarried – to her late husband's younger brother. Financially, this helped the family but then problems arose for Alchemist.

> *"My uncle, now married to my mother, started showing interest in me, sexually. He touched me inappropriately on several occasions and I told my mother, but she wouldn't listen. She didn't want to know."*

The fierce independence which was to become a hallmark of Alchemist's life then showed itself. She left home.

Her mother was astonished at Alchemist's action. But one thing she did realise was that Alchemist was rather more grown-up than she'd imagined; independent-minded and determined. Both Alchemist and her mother were surprised at her inner strength.

> '*My step-father's sexual interest in me was not something I made up or imagined. Or claimed out of hatred for him. It happened, it was true. That my mother never supported me in this awful situation just left me shattered.*'

Eventually, her mother did realise the truth of what had happened to Alchemist and she divorced the stepfather so as to provide Alchemist with a loving home, despite it being brutally impoverished.

> "*This experience gave me one of my first life lessons: people's cowardice and indifference are not always an indication of their true nature. They may react in a way you find unacceptable but are doing so out of temporary pressure or from social appearances sake. Beneath the bad behaviour may be a protective and loving core. This lesson taught me not to judge people too harshly too quickly.*"

Many teenagers would have crumbled under an early onslaught of such pain, disappointment, shame and poverty, so whether Alchemist was lucky or not is a question only she can answer. But in telling herself she was lucky, when self-evidently life had already dealt her a good dose of pain, Alchemist reveals another aspect of her inner character – her positive self-love.

University

The eighteen-year-old young woman who entered the finest university in the country was not the same young woman who, five years previously, had suffered the acute embarrassment of public menstruation. She was maturing fast and along the way recognising how social conventions limited her possibilities and those of women everywhere. She was not about to get on a soapbox and start preaching revolution, but neither was she going to accept the gender status quo.

> "*I was still young and had a lot to learn but what I knew already was to be my own person, my own woman. It wasn't easy. As far as being feminine was concerned, I didn't present it. I looked independent and not needy of anyone but inside I was still a woman. I was no conventional beauty and I never tried to be. I rarely used make-up and when I did it never looked right on me. Just messy. I was heavy-built and broad-shouldered. In fact, I looked quite masculine, still do, though I knew I was heterosexual. I'd long gotten used to being called 'ugly' at school but now at university I found a greater acceptance. I was able to begin forming my own identity as a woman.*"

Programmed by conventional norms of beauty, many relatives and friends casually and absentmindedly told Alchemist that "she was too ugly to be chosen by any man at all". Immature and innocent, she'd internalised that message during childhood. Coming to university, she learnt to find her own measurements of beauty, set up her own norms, look at herself through her own lens and create her own beautiful image. She accepted she was beautiful in her own eyes, in her own ways. Alchemist fiercely and vehemently validated herself from this point on, building up her self-confidence.

Alchemist had been accepted to do a degree in Education and Sociology. She was aiming to be a teacher and hopefully go into school leadership. But she remained poor. Intellectually, she'd left her family behind years ago, but she still needed money. Fortunately, she got the first in a series of scholarships and spent the next four years completing her BA and PGCE.

In her second year at university, Alchemist starts benefiting from her education and teaching skills: she does private tutoring and is now, at last, slowly becoming financially independent.

Her first full-time teaching job saw Alchemist working in another part of the country, a large university town near the coast. She had her own apartment and a steady income. What she was missing, however, was something much more personal – a male partner.

> *"Sex had become an important part of my self-identity but being a woman meant always considering how one was seen and perceived in terms of sexual mores. As much as I rejected this value system I still had to be mindful of it, especially as school teacher. I had a few male friends in my first couple of years as a teacher but then I met Alan."*

Marriage

Alchemist is no virgin when she meets Alan, a teacher working in a different school – she actually crossed her sex Rubicon in high school, while university life gave her further opportunity to learn more about sex and her sexual identity. Now, at the age of twenty-three, Alchemist feels she is ready for something more permanent.

> *"Alan was ten years older than me and divorced with a young child. I didn't mind that. I wanted an older man, someone with experience of relationships. All my partners up until then had been nearer my own age. I liked his confidence and I knew he was a good*

> *teacher, very professional. I think I saw how he was progressing as a teacher and respected him for that."*

Being well aware of her own emotions and needs, rejecting the conventional norm prescribing that the man should be the one who makes the first step, Alchemist was the one who first declared her love for Alan.

> *"At the time I imagined I loved Alan but looking back I can see two things shaping my behaviour. The first was the need for a family, to belong to something bigger than just myself. The second was physical need. I wanted regular sex, intimacy, closeness with a man and Alan provided that. Of course, with us both being teachers that gave us a lot in common, but really I didn't know who I'd actually married until after the marriage."*

The professional compatibility between Alchemist and her husband was important but what drove the relationship was sex. The sexual energy between them was immensely strong and deeply satisfying for both. Unfortunately, this aspect of their marriage proved to be the breeding ground for an altogether less joyful experience for Alchemist.

> *"Alan had concealed an aspect of himself which didn't appear until several months after our marriage. Basically, he was a sadist. He got sexual pleasure from seeing me in pain. This aroused him. He had one peculiar trait which was that he wanted my vagina to be dry when he penetrated me, so that it would be tight for him and painful for me. He would even wipe my vagina before sex to make sure I was dry. In the beginning I accepted this, I just thought it was quirky, a phase he'd get through. But it got more serious with him wanting to beat me and abuse me during sex. And then his bullying and violent behaviour in bed spilled over into our domestic life. That was when I knew I had to leave."*

Aside from physical sadism, Alan enjoyed making Alchemist suffer emotionally. He continually told her she was ugly, that no other man would take her – comments designed to make her to cling on to him, thus giving him the satisfaction of being important and significant in her life and in the marriage.

Alchemist needs a man in her life but not at any price. She has her dignity and self-esteem to protect. Already, Alchemist has suffered more than enough indignation in her life, she is not about to put up with it from an abusive, sadistic, bullying husband. Her husband knew Alchemist's weak spot – sexual pleasure. He then used it to try and dominate her, control her and weaken her resolve so that she'd submit to him. It didn't work.

However, before Alchemist could depart from the marriage she got pregnant, though this didn't stop her planning her exit.

> *"Alan and I were together a total of six years but for most of that time we were living apart. Within eighteen months he'd got a job in an international school in Dubai and I was looking to do an MA abroad. Our son was born and when he was eighteen months he went to live with my sister. I went to the UK to do the MA.*

One aspect of self-love which people may have difficulty reconciling themselves with is selfishness. Or, less pejoratively, an intention to put oneself first in most situations. It may not be considered a pleasant trait but it is important because it serves to protect the individual; it removes the risk of them living their lives for someone else – instead they live it for themselves. Which means they act with agency but must also assume the consequences of those actions.

For men such as Alan, putting themselves first and their child second didn't attract any social criticism. But not so for women like Alchemist. This is when self-love conflicts with social conventions over motherhood and filial duty.

> *"Sure, my family were not that impressed that I intended to go and live in the UK for a year and do an MA in Education, leaving my son with my sister, but I had been offered a scholarship at a leading university and there was no way my child could accompany me. It was a one-time opportunity and I had to put myself first in order to grasp it."*

Alchemist is twenty-seven when she returns from fifteen months in the UK, an MA graduate. Alan is still abroad with no intention to return, so they readily agree to a divorce. Alchemist resumes full-time teaching – but not for long.

> *"Doing the MA was a major test for me. I had to stretch myself intellectually, but the feeling of empowerment and satisfaction was great. Even before I'd finished the MA I was already thinking of a PhD."*

Within six months Alchemist has submitted a doctorate proposal to the same UK university where she did her MA, together with an application for a scholarship. She is accepted.

"I wanted to take my son with me but the UK student visas laws made that difficult, so he continued to live with my sister and her family...I was in almost daily contact with my son while in the UK"

This fractured upbringing experienced by her son would come back to haunt Alchemist in the years ahead, but right now she was focused only on her doctorate – and a yearning that is getter wilder and wilder inside her.

The Yearning Time

The pain and suffering from her traumatic marriage have left Alchemist emotionally bruised but not removed that most primitive of human cravings from within her; the need for sex, sexual pleasure and a satisfying relationship.

There are any number of ways to approach dating but in the twenty-first century they invariably start and end online. Alchemist, now living in a large UK city and fully into her doctorate, has desire, intent, opportunity and access to the internet.

"The doctorate was tough but it didn't take up all my time. My marriage was over, I was living in a different country with a more open cultural attitude towards sex and dating for women. I just adopted it."

Alchemist did more than simply 'adopt' local sexual values; she mingled them with her yearning for a soul deep connection, and then strategised them.

"I registered with over twenty online dating sites and simply posted my profile on all of them. Then I sat back and waited for the responses from men."

At this point in her life, Alchemist is demonstrating the inner resolve and calculation that has so far taken her from a desperately impoverished, near hopeless upbringing, to a PhD in the UK. In the beauty stakes, Alchemist doesn't feature hardly at all, but in the intelligence and confidence stakes, she is at the top. She has a strong physical desire but she is not ashamed of that desire. She does not suffer from guilt or a loss of self-esteem from wanting sex with men.

"I dated numerous men and came to each rendezvous with the same wild yearning as if it was the first time in my life. I longed

*for the man with equally deep yearning in his heart and equally
wild craving in his body. I believed that the man did exist and was
looking for me too."*

Alchemist is now in control of her life, at least as much as she can be. She is
thirty, living in a way which suits her, even if it doesn't suit everyone around
her. She acknowledges and embraces who she is as a woman, including her
sexual identity. She rejects sexual stereotypes that state that women should
be passive in seeking sexual partners. Alchemist creates her own sexual
norm – serial monogamy – and sticks to it strictly. This attitude and lifestyle
makes some people uneasy but all she is doing is adopting a masculine
approach to sex and relationships.

Men continue to come and go from Alchemist's life, and her bedroom,
but then two years into the PhD something happens that changes her life.
She meets 'the one'.

Househusband

In her third decade, Alchemist can already claim to have experienced a
good range of emotions, though a soul-deep love is not one of them. So
when it does hit her the impact is profound.

> *"I met my second husband online. He was from my country and in
> the UK doing a Masters. We lived in the same area so it was easy
> to connect. It was real love from the start and at that point my life
> really changed for the better."*

Despite falling deeply in love, Alchemist remains firmly grounded. She
is not about to throw her self-esteem, self-sufficiency and independence
overboard for this or any man.

> *"He was perfect for me in so many ways. Both of us were imperfect
> and we both considered our desires sacred. We created our own
> unique relationship blend and it has continued like that for the last
> ten years. He understands me and loves me for who I am. He is not
> on a mission to remake me into a more passive wife."*

On returning to their home country, the couple get married. With Alchemist
now holding a PhD in Education and her husband an MBA and working in
HR, Alchemist decides not to return to classroom teaching but to apply for
a post in the local Ministry of Education as a development officer. She gets

appointed. With two full-time incomes coming into the household, she is financially stable for the first time in her life.

Within two years, the couple have a child – a boy – during which time Alchemist and her husband have created a truly equal relationship, one based on gender preferences rather than gender stereotypes.

> *"I was now on a major career path in the Ministry of Education and my husband wasn't happy in his work. So we agreed he'd become a househusband. He is full-time at home. He does a little consultancy, part-time, but most of his days are taken up with childcare and domestic duties. He loves it."*

The man that Alchemist has married is a progressive. He has a liberal outlook on life, is emotionally intelligent, self-aware, and has the quality of self-love which means he doesn't feel insecure or inferior to Alchemist, or anyone else, on account of him being a househusband. He has gender confidence in himself as a man. He is secure in his masculine identity.

> *He is a Buddhist, like me, practises meditation and is aware of the toxic elements in life – greed, ignorance and anger. He always validates me, always reminds me when I get stuck in negative thoughts. He is my healer."*

This type of man is very different to Alchemist's first husband, a more toxic male, a man who needed to control a woman in order to feel comfortable within himself, a man who got pleasure from domination.

This gender-role reversal works perfectly for both of Alchemist and her husband. Though they are the only couple among their close friends and family who have adopted this lifestyle they see more and more couples following suit.

> *"Two of the women I work with in the Ministry have househusbands and many of the young single women I talk to say this is the sort of relationship they are looking for. It is still quite uncommon in my country but the trend is definitely towards a liberalisation of gender roles. It makes sense. I can earn a lot more than my husband and he prefers to be with the children rather than sitting in a corporate office, attending endless meetings."*

Life for Alchemist is perfect. Though as life has already taught her – it is rarely smooth for long.

Son

We all have those moments, those experiences which never leave us; when we can recall every minute, every second, with life suddenly in slow-motion as the impact of what we are seeing and hearing creates images destined to remain vivid in our minds forever.

"It was a sunny Sunday afternoon in June. My husband and I were enjoying a picnic in the park, with our seven-year old son. I was feeling relaxed after a busy few months at work. We were laughing and joking. We were actually trying for a second child and feeling very loving and romantic about that. Then my mobile rang."

It was her sister.

"At first I didn't comprehend what she was telling me. I went into some sort of mental lock-down I think. The only word which kept going over and over in my head, which was hammering in my skull, was 'suicide'.

Alchemist's sixteen-year-old son had jumped off a building.

Nothing in Alchemist's life had prepared her for this. It was a terrible, inexplicable, irreversible tragedy. Her reaction was as dramatic as it was natural.

"I jumped and screamed 'No!' 'No! over and over again. I yelled at my sister telling her she was wrong, that is couldn't be right. I'd only seen my son the previous week and he'd seemed very happy. I was completely lost, utterly distraught."

Even Alchemist's robust mental health was overwhelmed by her son's suicide. She cannot set foot outside her home for two months. People look at her with severe judgement in their eyes and for the first time in her life, Alchemist is scared. Almost everyone accuses her of being a bad mother or her husband of abusing his stepson. This judgemental attitude magnified the pain inside Alchemist. She agonised over what she had done wrong, how she had let her son down.

I experienced depression for the first and only time in my life. I went very low indeed. I didn't want to talk to or see anyone. My husband took the brunt of it, unfortunately. But he was very calm, very supportive. I couldn't have gotten through it without him... But what can you say? I couldn't change anything. My life had gone down a particular path and to be fair it was a path I'd chosen. My son had been living with his father some weeks, and with me other weeks. It seemed a good arrangement for everyone, it had been like that for years."

The inquest into her son's death confirmed suicide, though no reason was given. He'd had some unpleasant experiences at school regarding social media bullying, and had periods of being very melancholy, but to commit suicide was never considered a possibility.

Alchemist goes through the various stages of grief, including a period of self-loathing over being an absent parent. But she also knows this grief can never be totally exorcised. It will remain with her all her life. So she does what she's learned to do when faced with emotional pain: she accepts it and allows it to linger in her heart. She learns to live with it rather than try and deny it. She goes to sleep and dreams of her son, she works through the day with her son's presence always close and she is reminded of him constantly.

There isn't going to be any absolution for Alchemist. And nor does she expect any.

Alchemy

Are some people born lucky or is luck something we conjure up for ourselves? Certainly, this was a question Alchemist was now asking herself. And she was never able to come up with a good answer. Looking at her life one way, she'd been incredibly fortunate – a happy and contented second marriage, scholarships to top western universities, healthy children, good health for herself, and a blossoming career. But from another angle, life had dealt Alchemist some pretty awful cards; a childhood of humiliation and hardship, a disastrous first marriage, and now, worst of all – her eldest son's suicide.

And it wasn't over yet.

Months after the death of her son, Alchemist is pregnant for the third time in her life. When she found out she was going to have a girl then you can imagine the thoughts running through her head. She and her husband prepared a special nursery, finding renewed pleasure and remittance from grief in planning for this most welcome arrival to the family.

Their little girl was born almost exactly one year after the suicide of Alchemist's son. She lived for seven days only.

"I thought I had reached rock bottom the year previously, but there was more pain in store for me. Losing my baby daughter was

beyond words. I can't say more about it. I can't. It is still raw inside me and always will be."

There is no set script to follow when life throws you into a chasm of heartbreak. Every person finds their own way out, or they don't. And that is the challenge, to even bother climbing out of that chasm. Because someone like Alchemist would be entitled to ask herself 'why bother?'. Why indeed? If life has more pain and unbearable anguish in store for you, then what is there to live for? Where is the hope – because hope is one of life's nourishments. Without it there is only a cold bleakness.

Alchemist looked the cold bleakness in the eye and did not flinch. She did not become morose and depressed; she looked at what life had given her already and she knew one thing for sure – she was not giving up the beauty and love in her life.

"How many times have I had to face awful situations and how many times have I overcome them? Too many to count. And that is what gave me the most strength – I knew I could overcome. I knew my inner capacity for survival. I would allow myself to grieve, now over two lost children, but I would not repress that grief. Let it out. Own it, that was my approach."

Of course, Alchemist was not alone in her despair. She had a supportive husband.

"My husband is tall and strong, I call him my gentle giant. He is my emotional support, protective of me, and in his own quiet way he healed me with his unconditional love."

Alchemist is tenacious; she doesn't give up. She is also optimistic. For her, the glass is always half-full. And she is fortified by having experienced pain and overcome it. Allied with her devoted husband, she was able to slowly move on to a better place, a calmer, more tranquil emotionally comforting mindset.

The alchemy she performed turned the pain into resolution. She gradually transformed the worst possible experiences into learning experiences.

The process of self-torture and then self-healing repeated itself every day until the anguish began to reduce and the healing intensified. Eventually the day came when she could leave the pain behind. Her heart had grown large, soft and warm enough to be her own safe haven, her own inner home. The scar from the pain turned her heart into a wonder of warmth, protection and tolerance. Her inner strength enabled her to become a better professional, a more empathetic leader. She became fully liberated from gender and social conventional norms that dictate how a woman should behave or what a woman is.

> *"I spent a lot of time reflecting, thinking, being deep inside myself. I stopped torturing myself for not being a perfect mother. I acknowledged that I had tried as hard as any good mother would have that circumstance. I recognised my strengths and used them to fortify my resolve. I didn't ignore my weaknesses but neither did I allow them to dominate my sense of who I was. In the end, I came back to holding myself in highest regard. That saved me."*

Where Is She Now?

Wave upon wave of pain, crashing into the rock that is Alchemist, not all at once in a sudden deluge but periodically since birth. A form of torment – having to live with these waves of anguish; not knowing when they will come, how they will come, but being sure they will come. After the suicide of her son the pain was non-stop, day and night. Sometimes she would suddenly burst into tears and cry for hours. The pain surged up unexpectedly, wrenching her gut, depriving her of all physical and emotional strength.

These waves of agony swept Alchemist into the chasm but she didn't drown. She hung on to her self-worth, self-esteem and self-love.

And more than this, she became a better person, a worthier woman. Like any good alchemist, she turned worthless metal into gold, trauma into strength and agony into joy. The pain tortured her but into a much kinder, much more tolerant and kind-hearted person.

> *"I learnt to have sympathy and care for others, especially those who had lost a child or beloved. I found it in my heart to be more empathetic, with a stronger desire to protect people from sadness, disease, death. I started doing good deeds – for example donating blood on a monthly basis to help save kids in a big city hospital."*

She could have succumbed to toxic femininity; anger, bitterness, regret and self-loathing. She could have become a miserly and miserable woman. She didn't. Rather, she used all her life experiences, the good and the terrible, to create the woman she is today.

> *"I eventually did find out the cause of my son's death: innate disease of bipolar. At that point I stopped accusing myself. I stopped internalising other people's judgements. Things happen without any clear reason. No one is to blame at all."*

She now has a second child – a bright, bouncy and impressively healthy boy, twelve months old.

Her career in the Ministry of Education took off and she now leads a team of over a hundred, charged with inspecting schools and ensuring compliance.

Ask her staff about Alchemist's leadership style and you will get comments such as these:

"She is an inspiring leader"

"I love working for her, she is supportive and understanding."

"She operates a no-judgement system, and always encourages people to speak and have opinions."

"When I am a leader I want to be just like her."

"Without doubt, the best manager I have ever worked for... she empowers people"

Her marriage is stronger than ever. She and her husband make a point of sharing, communicating openly and validating each other.

Alchemist probably has her best career years ahead – she is still only forty-five. She will remain the family breadwinner, with her (house)husband in support, until she retires.

Her hair has turned pure white – physical evidence of years of hardship and struggle. It makes her look a lot older than she is.

"Why not dye my hair? Because it symbolises who I am, what I have become. I don't even wear make-up. I am proud of myself, my achievements. My hair turning white is my badge of honour, my achievement. I am not going to pretend to be someone I am not. Take me as I am, I love who I am, who I have become."

Life will likely have more surprises in store for her, hopefully all good ones, but no matter what the future holds, Alchemist is strong and experienced enough to handle it.

She is a remarkable woman, gifted with high intelligence. But determination, maturity, empathy, wisdom and resolve she has had to create for herself. No one handed her these traits at birth. She fought for them all the way. She created them out of trauma, pain and disappointment. She did so through self-love.

Alchemist has risen as a Goddess to become a woman whose heart is exceptionally warm and protective, soothing and tolerant. This alchemy has been created through pain and suffering. There are women like Alchemy around the world, each with a different story to tell. What they have in common are hearts that have a deep beauty and a fragrance that is beyond words, but which can be sensed by those who have either gone through the same process and possess the same hearts or who are blessed with that warmth.

When combined with a mind that is fierce enough to see through all the conventional limiting beliefs imposed upon women, wiping them all off the road, the result is an exceptional and precious human being.

And Alchemist has now taken a remarkable further step in her journey. She has become a mentor, friend and guide to others who have been hurt in relationships, have lost children or are experiencing agonising suffering. Alchemist acts to enlighten other women on the importance of rejecting social norms and judgements. She soothes hurting hearts and provides words of compassion and wisdom, but as a woman who has learned a lot about suffering, and about herself.

The world would be but a loathsome and cold place without the Alchemists among us.

Her scarlet heart
melts off
glaciers,

Her inner fire
burns off
limits,

Her Love torch
lights up
horizons…

Chapter Fourteen: Heart

RELEARNING HER ROLES, PERFORMING WITH PASSION

How many roles did you perform today? How many selves did you present to the world as you went about your daily business? For sure, it was more than one. A characteristic that makes humans a unique species is their ability to perform multiple roles, various presentations of self, all the while appearing whole, complete and undivided. Shakespeare's observation that 'all the world's a stage, and all the men and women merely players', is true enough. Though what Shakespeare didn't make clear is that men and women get to play many different types of roles during their lifetime; today perhaps Romeo, tomorrow Juliet, or even Cleopatra; maybe, on occasion, all three in the same day.

Some of these roles we will discharge with great accomplishment – the Oscar performances of our life, persuasive and convincing. Other roles will be best forgotten; to be consigned to our personal B-movie playlist.

Not even the greatest movie stars are great movie stars in every aspect of their life. They may be stunning on the screen, but not so wonderful as partners, parents, lovers or friends. And so it is with each woman and man – none of us can be winning Oscars every day for every role we are performing.

What distinguishes a brilliant performance from an abysmal one is passion – that ability to inject into the role and the performance, the essence of ourselves; our soul, our very heart.

Of course, there are some roles that demand a passionate response – the lover role, for instance. In this role if we are not performing with some passion then what is the point of it?

This story is about an ordinary woman who, from her teenage years, aimed to perform all her roles with passionate conviction. She came to bestride the stage of her life with intelligence, grace, compassion and beauty. If you were to meet her today you would be easily seduced by her artless charm, her unassuming manner and her joyful smile. What you would not see, however, are the wounds from past performances; the scar on her heart from a despondent love affair; the pain caused by a man who didn't have her resolve and who was unable to acquit himself as her leading man; and, not least, the price she paid for accommodating toxic femininity.

The Role of Daughter

From an early age Heart was able to witness close-up how one person can under-perform in one role, while shining out on another. That person was her father.

The eldest of three children, Heart grew up in a family of love and togetherness. Her mother and father were devoted to each other. Both were educated professionals, though only her mother held down a full-time job, as a teacher. She was pragmatic, dutiful and responsible. Heart's father was the dreamer – full of ideas of how to make money but lacking the ability to turn those ideas into reality.

> *"My father would sit me on his knee and read me fairy tales, stories of romance and great deeds. Then he would suddenly stop reading and say, 'you know, one day you are going to be very rich and have a beautiful home, just like the queen in this story. I am going to make sure of that."*

Heart's father never made good on his promise to provide her with material security. Instead he went bankrupt – not just once but three times during her first decade of life.

> *"I cannot remember how many times we had to move house while I was a child. I lost count, but it was many. All of my father's many businesses eventually failed. We never had financial security. Looking back, it seems my childhood was lived out in one financial storm after another."*

In her role of daughter, Heart learned a particular script. It meant staying quiet and getting out of the way whenever her mother and father argued, usually over money. And it meant learning the value of that which the family had very little – security. Heart, as a child, imbibed a keen awareness of the value of a healthy bank account.

This family stage had many settings. There was friction and insecurity, but also warmth and love. There was hope and optimism when bills got paid, and anguish and despair when the landlord kicked them out.

But unbeknownst to Heart, she was also learning a more dangerous narrative, one which taught how a woman must accommodate her man in order to keep the peace, in order to keep the family together. She was learning that wives should be compliant if not submissive, allowing their husbands to play at being masters of the universe.

Heart's father was no master of the universe, even though he hoped to be. He may have been loving but he was also weak and deluded. He saw himself as the dominant patriarch of the house, the male breadwinner entitled to put the family at risk so that he might pursue his dreams of success. What Heart saw was not just a failed businessman of a father, but a wife who accepted this situation. A woman who extended patience even in the face of despondency and hopelessness.

The best actors are adaptable. They can perform any type of role in any type of setting. Heart's father was not such an actor. Despite his unwavering ambition, he never learned the lines that bring about material success as a businessman. And those lines he learned in his father role, despite being words of love for his children, merely reinforced in them, and especially in Heart, the toxic masculine belief that husbands must be accommodated by their wives.

Heart was for sure learning a new script – toxic femininity.

"Even today, decades later, whenever I am with my father and mother I find myself slipping back into my childhood patterns of behaviour, my youthful responses to my father's character and my mother's acquiescence. I start to accept their reality, their particular relationship construct. Yet much of my adult life, especially in relationships, has been spent dealing with the toxic consequences their reality imposed on my perceptions of how a good wife should behave."

The Role of Student

The upheaval of never having a settled home life might have overwhelmed many young people, leaving them demotivated to study for higher education. Not so with Heart. She welcomed the daily routine and intellectual focus that studying required of her. It allowed her to slip out of the domestic chaos and into the workaday requirements of learning. She found a particular talent for languages and mathematics. Her home life had also given her another lesson – that if you want to go into business then you had better be well prepared. Her first choice was therefore to study business and management. She got accepted to one of the leading universities in her country.

The first year Heart spent at university saw her father succumb to yet another bankruptcy, the family having to uplift and move home once again.

Fortunately, Heart at least had the comfort of knowing her own home was secure – she was in university accommodation.

> *"I can only talk about a family home in the emotional sense. Because we never had a proper family home, physically. We just seemed to be constantly on the move, my father playing out whatever rags to riches dream was in his head at the time, my mother run ragged trying to hold down a full-time job and raise the kids. My first true physical home was my university studio apartment."*

One of the challenges that face many new university students is the move from a predictable if not stable family environment to the potential chaos of living on one's own. It was no challenge for Heart; she loved the feeling of independence and freedom. Going to university allowed Heart to leave chaos behind and instead create her own realm of safety and stability.

> *"Not only was university providing me with a secure living space, I was learning a lot of the stuff my father had little knowledge of – especially how to run a business. My degree was in business and management and I loved it. I was also learning Mandarin part-time as I could see an opportunity to provide translation services after I'd graduated."*

Learning Mandarin because she spotted an opportunity shows Heart practising for what was to become one of her starring roles – businesswoman. But that was still some years away. Looming up fast was an altogether different role – girlfriend.

The Role of Girlfriend

Influenced by her parents' relationship, Heart had, by the time she entered university, already begun to shape herself into a traditional femininity. Of course, she wasn't to know in her late teens just how toxic that femininity would become for her, she just saw it as the conventional norm for all women. She wanted to be loved and desired by a man and as she saw it to achieve such a state would mean submitting to him, pleasing him and putting him first. Just like her mother did with her father.

At the same time, Heart was also strong-willed and determined. This woman is no push-over. But like many women she is prepared to act out the role of weak, helpless, tolerant and always sweet woman in order to maximise her charm for a man. Heart is playing a role in order to appease fragile male masculinity, attract a man and keep him. Just as women have done down the ages.

> "I didn't feel like I was acting a role. I just was being myself. At least I thought I was. Looking back on my life I can now see how dangerous that role was for me. But it did bring me love – for a few years, anyway."

The love that Heart's role as a patient and passive woman brought into her life was for her overwhelmingly beautiful. She met her future husband during her third year at university. He was handsome, dewy-eyed, intelligent and Heart's dream guy. From the moment they first set eyes on each other at a friend's party they were rarely parted.

> "For both of us it felt like love at first sight. I had no experience of relationships, this was my first, but I didn't want any other man. Just him."

For the next seven years, Heart and her boyfriend are together constantly. Deeply in love, they hold hands whenever they are out walking, their relaxed physical intimacy natural and apparent to everyone. They rarely quarrel, their life is blissfully happy.

For Heart, this love is more than a physical and emotional attraction; it is a safe harbour from the continuing disruptions she experienced at home, as a growing child. Money worries are disappearing as both Heart and her lover are in full-time jobs. They are not able to afford their own home but the rent on their apartment is easily manageable.

And then the inevitable – they decide to get married.

> "Marriage was the obvious next step because we both wanted children. I was now in my late twenties and didn't want to wait any longer."

Within a few months of this decision, Heart is pregnant. Her husband suggests they leave the rented accommodation and move in with his parents so as to reduce their living costs and help with childcare.

> "That was the beginning of the problems. I didn't get on with his mother she didn't get on with me. There were a lot of arguments. It got to be quite stressful at times."

By the time Heart is thirty-three, she has two sons... and a failing marriage. The next two decades are spent attempting to manage this reality and to live with it.

The Role of Wife

The man Heart married turns out to be not so accomplished as a husband and father than he was as her boyfriend. With his mother covering childcare duties, he spends less and less time at home with his wife and young children and more time with his male friends, usually drinking. Then he gets made redundant.

> *"Suddenly, problems start building up for us. We have two children but money is now tight and I am having to work longer hours in order to maintain my career. I'm wondering what went wrong, what I did wrong. The closeness we used to have has disappeared. I feel forgotten."*

Very quickly, Heart's expectations of her husband get reduced dramatically. She no longer recognises the man she married, though she is not about to quit.

The role of wife under pressure from a failing marriage and feckless husband is not a role Heart volunteered for. How to respond? She decides to double down on being a passive, quiet wife. She learns to tolerate and adjust.

> *"I went silent, not shouting at my husband or my in-laws. I simply adjusted my expectations of him and them. It seemed the easiest way to deal with the situation. I didn't want endless rows. I had two children to consider and I'd experienced endless friction and family upheavals during my own childhood. I didn't want to impose this on my kids."*

Despite being out of work, Heart's husband is rarely at home or indeed out looking for a job. Instead, he begins a pattern of behaviour that persists for years – he lives off his wife and parents.

And then the sex escapades start to surface.

> *"What can you say when your husband starts coming home at 5 a.m. in the morning? Of course, I was thinking the obvious, though we were still having sex and that was important to me. I need that physical intimacy in my life. And I still loved him. I guess I closed my eyes and mind to what was happening in our marriage."*

Heart's married life is a bitter pill coated with a thick layer of sugar. But most of that sugar she provides. And she does so by not being resentful, by reducing her expectations of his responsibility, commitment, fidelity, financial contribution and housework share.

Heart's heart is filled with compassion and empathy; this is her natural way of being in the world. And she draws on that depth of emotionality to create a tolerable world for herself and her family. She is the source of all the emotional labour in the home; her husband is the one who draws on that source, always threatening to empty it through his cruel, distant, emotionally violating behaviour.

Heart's nights are spent mostly alone. Yet she yearns for physical passion. Her husband still occasionally satisfies that need in her, but not her need for warmth, love and companionship.

Is this the role of wife that Heart envisaged having to play out when she was a younger woman?

> *"No, of course not. But what can you do? Yes, I'm shattered by how my marriage has turned out, but I am still married and in my own way I still love him. And he loves me. But we've changed. Life has changed us. He is weak really. But he thinks he is strong. I have to let him think that. He is a man."*

One of the ways in which Heart manages her feelings for her husband is through pity. She actually starts to take pity on him, on his situation. Just like her mother took pity on her father and his endless series of failed business ventures.

This is the toxic femininity in Heart showing through in her attitude to marriage. She has become programmed to believe that women must be deferential to men, to be empowering of their husbands by being tolerant of their weaknesses and indiscretions. Heart doesn't challenge her husband to improve, to become the husband she once imagined he could be. Instead, she adapts herself, in the process becoming complicit in her husband's failing life.

While Heart is somehow able to put a blindfold over her eyes when it comes to her husband's behaviour, pretending the reality is something different, that is only how she is as a wife. It is not how she is in the other main role now emerging in her life.

The Role of Businesswoman

Heart may have pity for her husband but she is not about to have pity for herself. Despite the tests that life has given her she remains resilient and resourceful. And ambitious. Just how ambitious reveals itself during the long trough of her marriage.

The world that Heart grew up in was one where the principle of entrepreneurship, the willingness and ability to spot and seize a business opportunity, was firmly established. Notwithstanding her father's lack of ability to transform such opportunities into financial profitability, Heart recognises it's her only way to make money and duly create the material security she and her family badly need.

Several years before Covid-19 revolutionised online education, Heart establishes an online tutoring service specialising in languages and mathematics, her two favourite subjects. She starts small, with just a handful of part-time teachers operating in her city. Within a year she has created a nationwide business. When Covid-19 hits her country the demand for her quality online tutoring becomes so great she is able to quit her teaching job and become a dedicated businesswoman.

Over the next few years Heart expands her operation into all types and levels of online education, and then uses the profits to buy land and property. Today, she is seriously wealthy. She has rehoused her family into a large house in a prosperous suburb and paid off her father's many debts. Moreover, she has laid to rest the ghost of her father's multiple bankruptcies.

Heart is now performing the role for which is she most naturally suited. She has all the qualities required of an entrepreneurial businesswoman, but mixed with her emotional intelligence and compassion. She is not an authoritarian leader. On the contrary, life has taught her to be persistent but flexible, to know what her goals are but to have the confidence to swerve and change direction when looming up against a brick-wall.

> *"For me, being in business is fun. I love it. I enjoyed being a teacher but I didn't enjoy having to work with the education systems – they were tedious, restrictive and dispiriting. I think I'd always intended to follow my father into business, even though he experienced mostly failure. But I am not a workaholic. I have good management control of my various operations but I don't micro-manage people. I give them power and authority. This allows me to look for other business opportunities that might arise and to lead a balanced life."*

The rise of Heart the Business Woman changes the family's bank account but it doesn't change the family's emotional account – that remains firmly overdrawn. Indeed, the relatively sudden if not unexpected flow of money into the family coffers only serves to widen the gap between her failing husband and the successful entrepreneur which Heart now so self-evidently is.

"He became resentful. Even though I made sure he never went without money, I paid his debts, but he never appreciated it. He continued to live at home but really as a stranger."

The Role of Widow

There are many different types and levels of grief and various types of bereavement. As Heart has discovered, bereavement is not confined to physical death. Essentially, Heart's marriage started to die the moment it began. Now, over two decades later, it is totally dead, though not legally terminated.

Without realising it, Heart adapts once more to a new role, this time the role of widow. She has spent years trying to sustain the love for her husband, and done so despite his serial affairs, irresponsibility and absence of any warmth or care.

What starts as a subconscious sense grows into a fully conscious awareness that she is still married but no longer with a husband. She creates herself in a new image – the widow: without a husband but still with a wedding ring on her finger.

> *"I mentally left him. Physically, we haven't lived together in any intimate way for some years. But I needed to make the emotional, mental break. Create a separation from him in my heart. This I did. Having to focus on my business helped a lot. It was a joyful distraction from the heaviness of my marriage."*

Many wives would have kicked this man out years ago. Yet even today, Heart persists with supporting him. What does this reveal about her? Well, one might say she is soft, pliable and deluded. That she is her own worst enemy and should never have put up with an iota of the suffering her husband and his family inflicted upon her.

And yet there is the other side to it, the side which demonstrates Heart's nobility, her honour and duty to her family, especially to her two growing sons. She continues to believe that sacrificing her own happiness for the welfare of others is what it means to be a woman. And doing so gives her a powerful sense of identity validation – in her mind she is the woman she was raised to be.

Of course, the thread continuing to run through Heart's life is toxic femininity, the way she has been deeply programmed by a patriarchal society to put her own needs, as a woman, second to that of her husband. Conventional institutionalised toxicity has turned Heart into the victim of her own instinct to survive, her natural desire to be loved and cared for, her rational calculations and arrangements of her own private life, and especially her kindness and compassion. The stronger and more compassionate an individual she is, the more toxic she is feminine. She is too kind and forgiving for her own good – at least as far as her husband is concerned.

The level of toxicity of femininity within Heart is yet to be fully revealed. And Heart herself has little awareness of it. Until the Canadian enters her orbit.

The Role of Lover

The enchantment of love, being in love and receiving love from a man, was not over for Heart, even though she thought it was. For sure, there was no shortage of men interested in her. Heart was not just beautiful on the inside; she was beautiful in her soul and spirit. And she was wealthy, independent, interesting and educated. All she needed was a man who could be her equal, whom she could be devoted to, someone worthy of her love and her respect. But she didn't have the energy or inclination to go looking for such a guy. He would have to come to her. And eventually he did.

The moment came unexpectedly, during an education conference in Toronto. Being a leading online education business entrepreneur, Heart was invited to the conference.

> "I'd never been to Canada and I loved it. The country was amazing. So were the people. The conference lasted three days and during that time I met Jim."

Jim was also an educationalist, working in Vancouver, married with two children. His job took him around the world and he frequently visited Heart's country.

> "It was an immediate connection for both of us. We met on the first day and spent the rest of the conference in each other's company. I decided to stay on in Canada for another week which Jim and I spent touring Ontario."

During the course of that ten days with Jim, Heart falls deeply in love. She finds a depth of feeling for this man which she'd never felt with her husband. And she trusted Jim. Although he was married, he'd made no secret of that fact though explained that his marriage, like that of Heart's, was basically over. He was the 'widower' to Heart's 'widow'.

But how to sustain this love? How to create something long-lasting for both of them?

> *'Because of his senior position in the Ministry, Jim was able to get a posting to my country for nine months, to develop international education opportunities. It fitted perfectly for me. Within a few months of us first meeting he was living not too far away, in my city. We saw each other constantly. Did my husband know about our relationship? I didn't know and I didn't care. By then we had a tacit open relationship anyway. He did not figure in my life.'*

As the relationship develops Heart and Jim confront the issue of permanence. How to secure it. They are each committed to the other and recognise this is the big love of their lives. But their homes are thousands of miles apart. Someone will have to make a sacrifice. Who is it going to be?

> *"Towards the end of his time in my country, Jim asked me to marry him. I knew he would and I'd obviously given it a lot of thought. He'd brought a happiness and contentment into my life that I'd never before experienced. He was everything my husband was not. We would spend hours talking, just talking. There were never any arguments, mood swings, or unpleasantness. It was wonderful to be with him."*

Blissfully happy as she was, Heart didn't have the courage to take the decisive next step. She said no to Jim's marriage proposal.

> *"I just couldn't break up my family. I put them first, over my happiness. I constantly asked myself if I was wrong to do so but couldn't fully answer the question. I settled for continuity over joy."*

Jim went back home to Vancouver and his wife and family, deeply saddened at Heart's refusal to get married. They continued to communicate, but at a distance. Jim asked Heart a second time to marry him but she continued to refuse, though these refusals cost her a lot.

> *"I was in the most utter agony and pain. I was confused and feeling helpless. I couldn't sleep, I didn't want to talk to anyone. I barely ate. Although I was in love that beautiful feeling was tempered by the knowledge that I was going to lose Jim if I didn't agree to marry him. Online relationships are okay but he and I both needed more."*

161

Heart is now fifty years old. She has only had two men in her life. Both loved her, both she loved. But neither love has materialised into anything permanent. Both relationships promised much but for different reasons failed to deliver.

As a businesswoman, Heart is undoubtedly successful. Her businesses prosper and Heart need never worry about going bankrupt. Heart may be her father's daughter but she's the proven money-maker, not him.

As far as being a mother, Heart can hold her head up high. Her two sons are both now at university and doing well. They are the one blessing to come out of her marriage.

But in her roles as wife and lover, Heart has not achieved the joy and satisfaction she feels she deserves. Her memories of the men in her life are only good in parts. For Heart, there is no happy ending of everlasting love, romance and intimacy.

So, is Heart faced with living with regret and disappointment in terms of relationships for the remainder of her life?

Her father suffered serial bankruptcies. Is Heart fated to suffer serial failed love affairs?

Or is there a redemption role she can perform?

The Role of Self-Aware Woman

When an actor walks onto the stage or film set, she or he must know their lines. And so it is with humans, performing on the stage of life. We humans are given a script, a narrative, one linked to a specific role and this is what we perform, even while we are unaware it is just that, a performance.

And why is it a performance?

Because there are countless scripts for the same role. Being a mother, wife, husband, lover, sister, worker, boyfriend, brother or father, don't all come with the same script. We each may draw on a script but we also have the opportunity to write our own. We each create our own performance. Or at least we should.

From this arises individuality, agency and self-determination.

Many children may be force-fed a narrative or way of thinking from birth, but as adults they can acquire the intelligence, education and experience to step beyond the script. To become self-aware.

Following the break-up of her love affair with Jim, Heart tumbled into the depths of despair. Her natural optimism deserted her. She saw no future for herself, at least not a future filled with romantic love.

And then she stopped desiring. She stopped fighting her inner conflicts and embraced her contradictory emotions.

> "I read books on spirituality, religion, especially Buddhism. I started to do meditation. I spent a lot of time talking to women friends who'd also gone through divorces and failed love affairs. I came to realise that the problem was rooted in my desire for love. In my sense of not being complete as a woman without having a man in my life who loved me. I came to realise that this desire was actually toxic and not beneficial for my wellbeing. I had for too long tolerated an intolerable situation with my husband – out of fear of being alone. But then when a man came along who was worthy of my love I denied him. Why did I do that? Because I privileged the role of wife and mother. I actually should have dismissed these roles altogether and simply existed as my own person, my own being.

Where Is She Now?

Regarding her marriage, Heart has a achieved a minor miracle. After more than twenty years, her husband and her in-laws have come to recognise who Heart really is: that she is kinder than them all, warmer than them all, more tolerant than them all, and surely stronger than them all in a variety of aspects. She has gained their respect and awe, in the most organic and noble manner. It is a soft but powerful gender role revolution that Heart has done to her marriage. It takes a very strong will, steel resilience and a diamond heart to accomplish it.

- Her husband no more dares to look down on her as someone he can manage.

- Her husband is grateful for her financial support, and finds her heart the best shelter for his life.

- He now does more than his share of housework and shows more care towards the kids and his in-laws.

- Her husband's male ego is humble and is healthier for it.

Heart is still the tacit widow and she will never love her husband as she used to. But today she feels complete inside, satisfied with her life and adjusted to her reality. Love may yet come forth for her. She is actually more beautiful than ever, giving off an aura of warmth and empathy. But she can live without such love if she has to. Heart has become her own woman, not the woman demanded by the various roles in her life.

How Did Heart Achieve This Breakthrough?

Husband sees a wife, children see a mother, employees see a boss, parents see a child, lover sees a soulmate. Which of these was Heart's real role? They were all real and yet none of them were real.

These were performances played out on the Shakespearean stage of life, some more successfully than others. But all acted with passion and conviction.

Yet none of these roles were really Heart. It took her over four decades to reach inside herself, discover herself, become her own woman, touch and have confidence to display her essence. Until then she was still trying to read the script correctly, to play the responsible wife, the dutiful mother, the worthy child, the good boss and the desirable lover.

Heart continues to play the roles expected of her by family, friends and employees, but now she does so aware of the woman behind the roles. She came to recognise herself, nurture that self, and love that self.

The breakthrough came in three ways, all triggered by Heart's advancement in emotional intelligence and self-love – **her emotional development**:

Eliminating or Dismissing Disappointment, Resentment, Anger

Disappointment, resentment, anger, and hatred towards people, incidents and circumstances often arise from the discrepancy between our expectations and the external reality. These expectations stem out of our past experiences, memories and the conventional norms that we have internalised. In numerous cases, these negative emotional reactions towards reality cause more suffering than the undesired reality itself. To do away with these negative emotional reactions can effectively lessen the sufferings.

To eliminate negative emotional expectations, Heart has learnt to…

1. be aware of them, acknowledge them as normal and natural, and tolerate their presence in her mind.

2. dig deep into her memories, past experiences, and internalised norms and see the emotions that lie beneath them and then embrace them with love and care. Once the emotional root is removed, the past memories and experience will shrink in size

and intensity, leading to a less negative response to the external reality.

3. analyse the discrepancy between the external reality and her expectation, so as to shift her interpretation of reality into the most accurate version, and then stick to it, rather than holding on to an illusion of reality. For example: as soon as she adopted and embraced the role of 'widow' her emotional sufferings lessened remarkably. She effectively compartmentalised her husband and her marriage; accepted the reality and was able to move on with her life.

Managing or Dismissing Desires, Cravings and Needs

To eliminate and control her desires, Heart has learnt to…

1. Acknowledge the existence of her desires as a natural part of life. Every single human being is a bundle of numerous needs and desires which stem from the five senses, the physical body and individual psychology. In most cases, the desires and needs are indicators of good health. Trying to do away with them is futile. The thing to do is to embrace them and the healthiest response is to be grateful to their existence.

2. Recognise that a large proportion of her desires and cravings are not what she actually needs. So many of one's desires and cravings contradict each other. Identifying them, putting them into their place in the whole picture of her life is a very effective way for Heart to filter them, keep some and eliminate others. This allows her to enjoy more tranquillity and peace, and avoid many unnecessary traumas and sufferings.

3. Consider satisfying herself if a desire is healthy, reasonable and feasible. Otherwise, she will try to acknowledge the desire, embrace it in her tolerance and love, and finally assimilate it into her love force.

4. Mix self-management and self-discipline with self-love: Heart realises she can stay happy and fulfilled without having all her needs and desires satisfied.

Spiritual development – the inner journey

To journey into her inner self, Heart has learnt to…

1. Differentiate between casual, merely physical connections and soul connections (which she enjoyed with Jim). Heart had momentary physical satisfaction from sex with her husband but the soul connection she enjoyed with Jim was far deeper and more satisfying. The former can physically satisfy one for a while but the latter brings about long-lasting fulfilment and allows the soul to blossom with joy and sweetness.

2. Shift from living a merely physical and material life into a more soulful one. Heart has experienced a relatively unconditional wellness rendered by doing meditation and transforming her emotions, which brings about an air of youth and a look of joy on her face, making her strongly attractive to her colleagues, friends and acquaintances, both male and female.

3. Understand that what allows her to make this spiritual and emotional development is her resilience, her kindness and compassion – thereby reinforcing her independent femininity.

4. Understand that her weaknesses, mistakes and toxicity have actually led her to be more in touch with her inner self. She used the pain in her life for self-development.

5. Appreciate that while she has been successful at being financially self-sufficient, she is now learning to be emotionally self-sufficient.

Heart used to be attractive to toxic men such as her husband precisely because of her toxic femininity, her traditional way of being a woman. Men saw a woman who was desirable yet compliant, submissive and passive. This allowed them to feel dominant and superior to her. It allowed them to imagine they could control her. It therefore validated their own toxic masculinity – their need to be the ascendant partner in a patriarchal relationship.

Heart is now attractive to those men (and women) who realise the emptiness of material and physical satisfaction, who are progressive in their attitudes towards gender identities and non-abusive ways of being in the world – enlightened individuals, such as her Canadian lover, Jim.

Heart has always been a woman of beauty, worthy of appreciation and entitled to love. Now that beauty is becoming more and more soulful. She is no longer acting out roles to appease others, but living as a woman full of self-love.

Amid countless
weaknesses,
confusions,
and
absurdities,

she touches herself—
beautiful,
powerful,
and
perfectly pure.

Chapter Fifteen: Silk

A Quiet Strength, A Gentle Power

How old were you when you experienced your first real emotional trauma? Perhaps you were in your teens or even childhood. A great many of us are. Certainly, it is not uncommon to have suffered a fairly traumatic event by the time we reach our mid-twenties. This seems rather cruel of life – to inflict upon the innocent and certainly the inexperienced, its harshest vicissitudes.

But maybe that is one of life's aims - to constantly test us and in the process teach us. Without ever truly knowing why we are here it is worth at least considering the possibility that we are here to learn.

And what better way to learn than through experience?

What better way to find our depths than through having to plunge them?

What better way to become stronger than through having no choice about it?

Few of us seek out trauma but no matter, trauma will find us. We can emerge from childhood blithely ignorant and starry-eyed, but that is only a temporary state. It must be if we are to survive. If we are to protect ourselves. If we are to grow.

Recognising such, some interesting questions get raised, one of which is what type of upbringing will best prepare us for the challenges which life is about to throw at us? We won't get this preparation in formal education – no curricula could manage it. And we won't get this preparation from spending all our time looking at a screen.

No, we have to live and living fully requires us to take the occasional risk.

This is where love comes in, because there is no greater risk than that which comes with love – not just losing a loved one but especially from falling in love with the wrong person.

In Silk's story, love has a key role – indeed two roles; it is the angel sent to guide and protect, and the villain sent to test and traumatise.

One in Ten

Silk's first life lesson was how to survive in a family of ten; eight children, of which she was the youngest, plus mum and dad. Not many youngsters nowadays have to learn such a lesson – they are likely to be an only child or perhaps have one sibling. Silk's eldest brother had already left home and was married with his own child when Silk arrived, the final but very welcome addition to the family.

By love, if not by necessity, baby Silk's is a close-knit family – physically because they all live in a small terraced house in a quiet town, emotionally because mum and dad bind the family together with love, affection, care and endless effort. What also binds the family is poverty. There are no luxuries, no trips to the shopping mall to buy designer goods and the latest device; only simple pleasures and hand-me-down clothes for all the children. Dad is a low-level council officer, mum is the homemaker. Neither parent went to university but they have loads of good values and common-sense. They are honest, dutiful and responsible. Where does this morality spring from? Well not from religion because this is not a religious family. Nobody prays and nobody worships. They merely support and cherish each other because that is the right and proper thing to do.

> "The word that most springs to mind when thinking about my childhood is harmony. We all got on, at least most of the time. Mum and dad were responsible and all of us admired them for that. Although there was no money, we managed. My parents taught that there was a good approach to life and foremost was to be honest, to be sincere, to be hardworking. Then good results would follow."

Such a principled working-class morality, sober and dignified in its austerity, absent of greed, selfishness and venality, may seem old-fashioned in today's world but it worked for Silk and her family. Moreover, it provided her with the template upon which to structure her life. It gave her self-discipline and resolve, patience and fortitude. This would prove a powerful value system, one she was going to need in the not-too-distant future.

The first impression you'd have received from meeting Silk when she was a teenager would be her ordinariness. Physically, she is no stand-out beauty. But nor does she try to be. She is cheerful and carries a ready smile wherever she goes, for whoever she meets. There would be no hint of anything more to her than a gentle, kind, innocent young woman. Even her voice betrays her – it too is so quiet as to be barely audible.

Her high-school teachers find her so unassuming as to be almost invisible in class. Until, that is, exam time. Then she rises above her peers. Silk graduates from high school with outstanding grades – this unlikely, diffident achiever turns out to be the most likely to succeed.

Stepping Out

Silk might be an A+ student but that alone won't guarantee her a place at university. She needs money, specifically the money for fees and living costs. Her country's education system provides little of both even to the best students. She must find that money herself.

At this point her family can no longer help her.

> "My parents were very clear – they had no money to pay my university fees and costs. I'd been offered a place to study chemistry and physics at the best university in the country but without money behind me is was just a dream. In fact for me, it became a nightmare. When my parents told me this I just cried for a month. I was heartbroken. I knew my life would be nothing without going to university."

This knock-back floored Silk for a while but not for too long. She decided to seek the help of a businesswoman, someone known for assisting promising female students. She was given her contact information by a supportive teacher. Unfortunately, to meet this woman Silk would have to travel to the big city and knock on her office door. In effect making one of the most important cold calls of her life.

> "I never told my parents. I just got on the bus and went. I did have a letter of recommendation from several of my teachers and my certificates. I was terrified, both of meeting this woman and of being rejected, but I had to do it."

Trying not to get too panicky and at the same time appear confident and calm, Silk makes her pitch to this businesswoman. The pitch is quite simple – please pay my university fees and I promise to work for you for five years after I graduate and at a reduced salary.

Her benefactor's business was cosmetics and organic food production and she was always on the look-out for skilled young scientists. A deal was struck.

"That meeting turned out to be one of the most important of my life. It set me on my career path...When I went home and told my parents they were astonished. Actually, they were rather angry at first. They said I'd taken charity. It was true, I had. But not for free. I'd simply done a deal with a businesswoman. Eventually, my parents saw the sense in it. Though I really think they felt guilty at not being able to help me, financially."

For the next four years, Silk devotes herself to studying, her life revolving around the university library, lecturers and seminars, and her apartment. She became close friends with other women students and so began to learn a little more about herself as a woman amongst women, not just as a daughter and student. She graduated with distinction.

Several threads of silk have now been added to Silk's character: determination, self-discipline, courage and ambition.

The Scientist

True to her word, Silk now starts her career working as a junior technician in the research and development laboratory of her benefactor's company. It is a good job, well-paid even with a deduction to help repay Silk's university debt. The work suits Silk's temperament – it requires concentration, robust analysis, patience and carefully applied research methodology. Silk is a scientist at heart and in her temperament.

"I like the cleanness and clarity of scientific research. It is simply a matter of test, analysis and deduction. There is little in it which gets complicated by human emotion. In a way, scientific research is pure and honest so long as one applies the correct methods."

Becoming increasingly dedicated to her work, Silk makes rapid progress up the company career ladder. Even though she is still in her early twenties, her boss invites her to join a small team doing training and development for another part of her organisation.

Although Silk does have social skills and enjoys joining her work colleagues for occasional dinners and weekend get-togethers, she is happiest in her own company, quietly reading or considering some scientific conundrum. So the thought of having to stand in front of her peers and talk about her research and also help with training, fills her with some anxiety.

"It was a big change for me. I hadn't considered that aspect of the job but neither could I refuse. The first night before I started this work I could hardly sleep."

There was another reason for Silk accepting this extra responsibility – her boss was offering her the chance to do a part-time MSc, all fees paid. Silk could hardly refuse that opportunity.

First Encounter

Training and assisting her colleagues in the techniques of scientific research becomes a regular aspect of Silk's work life. She is promoted to Second Technician and, at the age of twenty-three, is more financially secure than her family had ever been.

One of the members of a group Silk is training is a male technician four years older than her. At the end of one working day he asks Silk if she'd like to join him for an early dinner.

"Of course, I'd noticed him in the group and I could see him watching me quite intensely whenever I was speaking but perhaps I was at that time so wrapped up in my work, my job, that I didn't think any more about him."

Silk may not have thought about him, but he was definitely thinking about her and the invitation for dinner came just two weeks after she'd started working with him and his colleagues.

Silk had never had a relationship. She was completely inexperienced in matters of love, sex and romance. Her life, so far, had been dedicated to leaving behind her family's grinding poverty, creating opportunities for herself, getting educated and standing on her own two feet. But she had feelings. She knew she wanted male company. She had desires. In that respect she was no different to the young women she had studied with at university and the women she worked with.

"My women colleagues, at least the older ones who were married or in relationships, would often talk about their love lives, the men they were seeing, even sometimes about sex. I listened and was interested but I could hardly contribute. I knew nothing about men. I knew I wanted love and I felt sexual desire, but my relationship model was my family, my mum and dad. I wasn't going to go to bars and look for a man. I had to wait until the right man came along."

Innocence is dangerous, especially when it connects with young love. And yet losing innocence is a necessary part of growing up and maturing. At the age of twenty-three, Silk may have the intellect of a much older woman but in terms of love and sex, she is a child. This child is about to be given a lesson in life and in relationships she will never forget.

The young man who asks her out for dinner becomes a regular feature in her life. Indeed, he starts to occupy much of her mental space.

> *"My first reaction at his invite was surprise, but quickly followed by feeling flattered. I'd never dated anyone. I'd avoided all that at university – I was too scared of failing my degree to get involved with anyone. My studies came first. And then with my new job, that came first."*

Over the next few months, Silk and her young male admirer begin regular dating. He is handsome, sociable, dreamy eyed and, unbeknownst to Silk, very experienced with women. He knows all the techniques of manipulative love – looking into Silk's eyes as she talks; speaking and writing romantic words just for her; listening and paying attention to her; praising and flattering her; showing care and attention. He is seducing her. And she is willing him on, this man with no-name.

No-Name

> *"No, I won't say his name. I never speak it now. You can refer to him as 'no name'. You are asking me to remember and talk about the most painful time of my life. I will because I want other women to know what I went through and how I came out of it. But this man, in my mind and in my life, no longer exists."*

Marriage

Silk and No-Name spend two years courting. She remains a virgin during this time, committed to wearing white at her wedding for all the traditional reasons.

> *"I would have agreed to getting married sooner but by then I was also doing my MSc and that took two years to complete. It was a busy time for me. But also, a wonderful time. I felt I had everything – my job, a career path, financial security, my qualifications and, of course, my fiancé, who I loved deeply.*

As soon as Silk graduates from her Masters she and No-Name get married. It is a big, traditional wedding. His family pay for most of it.

Are there any doubts in her mind, as she walks up the aisle to get married?

> *"Not really, this was my dream come true. The only question in my mind was what would the sex be like. I was still a virgin. We had done heavy petting but no penetrative sex. I wanted sex. I was eager for love and romance, for spending nights in bed with my husband. All my needs and desires were focused entirely on him. But it was all still in my imagination. I'd talked to my mother about sex and marriage and gotten some advice from her but she and my dad had always loved each other and the physical side of their relationship arose out of that."*

There is one cloud on this otherwise pristine horizon and that is No-Name's family. No-Name inadvertently lets slip one day that his father has a mistress.

> *"That surprised me. They seemed such a happy couple. That his father had a mistress and as it turned out, had had a number of mistresses during their marriage, was so different to my dad. I didn't ask any more questions. But it lingered in my mind."*

Silk has her first experience of full sex on her wedding night.

> *"This was when my husband's experience of love helped our relationship. But only in the sex aspect of it."*

Sexually, the marriage is a great success, at least for Silk. She and her husband make love every night for the next three months and Silk relishes each passionate moment. At long last she feels a complete woman – happily married and content with her life, blossoming now within herself.

> *"The sex was for me, just like it was for my mum and dad – the physical expression of deeply felt love and tenderness. My love for my husband was complete. He satisfied every aspect of me, all my needs. I trusted him completely. I could see my future ahead; we'd have children after a couple of years, certainly by the time I was thirty. My job was secure, I had a career path opening up before me, and I had confidence in my ability to do well in life. Everything was perfect."*

Hell 1

There is a sort of absurdity in an inexperienced young woman falling in love and believing it will all go on happily ever after, for the remainder of her life. But this absurd notion is held by many millions of young women around the world. Perhaps it is nature's way of ensuring the reproduction of the species; if so, it is women who mostly suffer the consequences – they are much more likely to fall in love with the romantic ideal, ignoring the reality of divorce and separation, and ignoring the legions of disappointed older women. No doubt each young woman fervently believes she will be different, that her love will be more robust and that the man she loves will be faithful and true forever. They see marital hell in the lives of other women but never envision it for themselves.

Hell came knocking for Silk in the form of a note pushed under her door one morning when her husband was not at home.

"All it said was 'your husband is seeing another woman. She lives at ….. He is with this woman now.'"

When Silk picks up that note and reads it she crumples to the floor, just staring at the few words, words which have immediately turned her life upside down.

"I felt physically ill. My heart was pounding. I couldn't think. But was it true? Was someone playing mind games with me?"

Silk agonises over the message for an hour, then, unable to stand the turmoil in her mind any longer, dons her coat and drives to the address given in the note. It is a Saturday morning. Her husband is working overtime, so she thinks. She parks near the house and watches. She is in a state of confusion, whether to stay and possibly see the worst or to leave and ignore the note. She stays. Sure enough, her husband eventually emerges from the house. Any doubt in Silk's mind disappears when, just before leaving, he turns and kisses a woman with some passion.

"I went back home and to bed. Just lying there thinking. He got home later that evening. I showed him the note. Of course, he denied it. I told him I'd seen him at the door of the house, kissing the woman, presumably the house owner. Then he got brazen. Told me it was none of my business who he saw. That was the end of our marriage."

175

That moment marked the end of Silk's marriage but it didn't mark the end of Silk's pain. There was more to come.

After this revelation, No-Name walks out the house and moves in with his girlfriend, but not before he told her that he'd never been faithful in the marriage. That there had always been another woman during their brief three months of marital 'bliss'.

> *"No-Name was nothing more than a playboy. Why he married me I don't know. Maybe he wanted a virgin wife? I felt stupid, gullible. My self-esteem shattered. For a long time, I couldn't eat or sleep properly. I was utterly broken up."*

Silk thought she was broken but there was more to come.

> *"I started divorce proceedings immediately. My mum and dad, my whole family, were really supportive. His family were not. They accused me of being an unsupportive wife. They said the fact that my husband was unfaithful did not justify a divorce. His parents were angry with me, not with their son.*

Silk didn't realise it but she'd married into a family where toxic femininity and toxic masculinity lived side-by-side, nourishing each other. Her father-in-law was a serially unfaithful husband, emotionally abusive to his wife. Her mother-in-law had internalised that abuse as a normal condition of married life for women. She expected her daughter-in-law to conform, to also be passive and accepting. Silk was not to rock the marriage boat, and certainly to not demand a divorce.

But Silk was made of stronger stuff. She was not about to tolerate an unfaithful husband, a life of sheer hell, just because of her mother-in-law's toxic femininity.

Hell 2

From the moment Silk discovered No-Name's duplicity, her life is on hold. She cannot concentrate much on anything. She decides to reveal all to her boss, the woman who had helped her through university and whom she respected enormously.

> *"My boss's reaction was really supportive. She made sure No-Name was moved to another division in her organisation so that he and I could no longer encounter each other at work. Fortunately, he didn't appreciate that and resigned. That was the one bit of good news I was getting around that time. At least I wouldn't see him."*

But then another event occurs to create even more turmoil.

> *"One month after starting the divorce proceeds I found I was pregnant."*

Silk now has two extreme situations – an ongoing divorce and an ongoing pregnancy, both with the same man. Everything she has worked for and strived to achieve is now at risk. Her happiness, her contentment, her self-worth and her desire for a family.

At this point Silk wavers. She believes she is right in asking for a divorce but she is also prepared to follow the line of her mother-in-law if it means she can bring her child up in a family environment. In a moment of weakness Silk phones No-Name, tells him she is pregnant and expresses the desire to rekindle the marriage.

> *"He shouted at me down the phone, told me I was useless and demanded that I come to see his parents, beg for their pardon and forgiveness for filing the divorce. He told me it was my mistake and that I had to put it right."*

Silk refuses to apologise. Her self-esteem may be low but it has not disappeared altogether.

A week later No-Name turns up at her house with his father and brother. They have booked Silk into an abortion clinic and are demanding she accompany them to it.

> *"I had little choice. I was still living in the family home and my salary barely covered the mortgage. No-Name wasn't giving me any money. I had the divorce to sort out. I let these three men take me to some private abortion clinic and I had it done there and then. They waited outside the clinic until I'd had the abortion. No more baby."*

Six months later, Silk is a divorcee.

Aftermath

In the space of just nine months, Silk has gone from a beautiful wedding with the man she loved, a man she confidently expected to live the rest of her life with, to a bullied abortion and a bloody divorce. She is still only twenty-five.

Physically she is shattered. Her weight drops from 52 kg to just 40 kg. She looks haggard. She is skin and bone. Her doctor signs her off work and she doesn't return to full-time employment until after the divorce.

Emotionally, Silk is an even bigger wreck. Everything she believed in has come to naught. Silk is emotionally damaged so much she can barely think. She returns to live for a while with her mum and dad, spending time just reading, going for walks and trying to rehabilitate herself. Her family are not religious but the idea of an abortion is abhorrent to them. It is a very bitter pill for her mum and dad to swallow. But at least they don't blame their daughter. No-Name becomes the great unmentionable in the household. He is a ghost – ever-present but never acknowledged.

Silk cannot afford keep the home and anyway it is now filled with bad memories, so she sells it, enabling her to pay off the mortgage. At least her job is secure and this is what she focuses upon during the next five years – because that is how long it takes her to resurface into something like normal living.

The Five-Year Resurrection

When a person experiences trauma it is usually the mind more than the body that is affected. The body may well heal in time but minds often never fully heal. Silk faced a level of emotional upheaval she could never have imagined and for which she was wholly unprepared. On the contrary, just a few months prior she'd been enveloped in marital bliss so to suddenly be thrown into her personal abyss of grief and betrayal was almost too much for her to cope with.

Over the course of the coming months and years, Silk has to process several, mostly unanswerable, questions and dilemmas.

Q. What did I do wrong?

Silk believed she'd done all the right things in her marriage, in her relationship with No-Name. She couldn't see how she'd come to deserve this treatment. In her mind, it was all utterly unfair to her. Her mind could not produce an explanation for his betrayal due to her being inexperienced in love and relationships and having little or no proper understanding of men.

Memories of their love and marriage haunted her day and night, and often hit her unexpectedly and at rapid speed. She spent endless hours trying to rationalise No-Name's brutality and that of his family but couldn't come up with any explanation.

Q. Why wasn't I a good enough wife?

Silk was torn between self-blame and hatred for Non-Name. Which emotion she felt at a particular time could depend on any number of factors

– for example, watching a TV movie and seeing another woman experience infidelity and observing how she dealt with it; unexpectedly hearing a song on the radio that she and No-Name both liked to listen to and finding waves of emotion washing over her; or simply waking up in bed and missing his physical presence, aching with pain and loss. She looked for answers to this question online, in social media groups and in reading other women's accounts of broken marriages. She looked for answers within herself, especially her lack of experience in relationships and sex. And then there was the woman herself, the one No-Name had left her for. She found out about her online and read her social media posts. But this only confused Silk more – the woman was uneducated, plain looking, and a divorcee with two children. Surely, Silk was more worthy of his love, not this other woman?

Q. How can I get revenge?

As Silk slowly starts to compartmentalise her strongest emotions, enabling her to begin healing, there remains one emotion which won't easily disappear – the desire for revenge. She knows she cannot answer the question 'why did this happen to me?', she just knows it did happen to her. As Silk sees it, she has come off worst in this breakup. No-Name is getting on with his life. That seems terribly unfair. But how to get revenge? What can she do to harm him? Does she even want to harm him? What would that say about her if she did embark on some lengthy campaign of revenge?

Q. Should I have stayed with him, apologised to his parents for wanting a divorce?

Of all the questions bubbling-up in Silk's mind, this one is the relatively easiest to answer. Silk may be confused and experiencing chaotic emotions, but one thing she does know very well indeed is this:

"*As much as I wondered about the abortion and whether or not I could have saved my child, I do know that I could never be in a marriage with an unfaithful man. I could not tolerate always being the third party, the wife-at-home, the cheated-upon woman.*"

All these questions and more generate constant mood-swings in Silk. Her thought-chains shift from one extreme to another, often in the space of a few minutes:

A feeling of being innocent and childlike ←→ A feeling of being a vengeful, hateful monster

A feeling of love and desire ←→ A feeling of
not wanting any man ever again

A feeling of confidence and pride ←→ A feeling of being stupid and gullible

A feeling of belief in her future ←→ A feeling of
bitter resentment at her destroyed life

A feeling of self-worth ←→A feeling of being
an utterly worthless individual

A feeling of self-validation at what she has overcome
←→ A feeling of guilt, shame, regret

The first year of resurrection sees Silk processing these feelings, experiencing them often without any control, and simply trying to pick up the threads of her previous life. She is a highly intelligent young woman, a scientist with a rational and logical explanation for most phenomena, but that rationality doesn't help her with this dilemma.

> *"As much as I tried, my brain couldn't produce a reasonable explanation for what had happened to me, nor for No-Name's behaviour. Were all men like this? No. My father wasn't. Was I too innocent? Yes, but am I to blame for being innocent and naïve? Was I too trusting? Obviously, but what is the point of marrying someone if you don't trust them? So much of what I was learning about me and about him, was hindsight. I didn't know any of this on the day I got married."*

For Silk, the real healing began when she got exasperated with her own brain.

> *"Eventually, I had to stop. I had to try and close down my mind, close down or at least reduce my constant mood swings, thought swings. It was all getting too much for me. I was already a physical and emotional wreck, but I couldn't carry on like that. It would destroy me and I wasn't going to let this man destroy me. That was the start of my healing process. I decided to get revenge on him by not getting revenge on him. By totally forgetting him, erasing him from my mind. Dismissing him as nothing, worthless. A No-Name."*

Erasing No-Name from her brain is one thing, erasing the constant thoughts from her brain is another. Then Silk reads about mantras; how repeating the same words or phrase over and over again can create a particular mental response – a sort of self-manifestation of reality.

> *"My mantra was very simple: 'no thinking'. I would repeat this over and over again whenever unwanted and destructive thoughts surged in my brain; no thinking, no thinking, no thinking, no thinking, no thinking...*
>
> *I would go to bed saying this mantra before sleep, I would say it anytime of the day. And for as long as I needed to. It became my mental tool, my emotional defence. It worked."*

Self-Love

Silk's five-year resurrection slowly but surely becomes a five-year self-validation, a journey out of hell and into self-love. Between the ages of twenty-five and thirty, Silk rearranges some aspects of her life and allows others to remain firmly in place.

> *Career:* Her work continues and she immerses herself in the relatively peaceful and knowable world of scientific research and discovery. Here at least, logical answers can be found to difficult questions.

> *Relationships:* There are none. Silk is far too bruised to allow herself to get even remotely involved with any man.

> *Family:* This is her main resource and site of emotional well-being. Whenever possible, and especially long weekends and holidays, she spends with her family. No one mentions the past. They don't need to. No one is critical or judgemental. Her family are completely non-toxic, totally loving and compassionate.

> *Friends:* Women's friendship becomes another important resource for Silk. She nurtures old friendships and cultivates new ones, both online and face-to-face. She makes time for friends and they make time for her. She learns more about herself and being a woman by sharing her feelings and experiences with her women friends.

> *Home*: Silk's new home is a small rented apartment. it is not luxurious but it is her space. Her private domain. It is where she feels safe even though she is alone most of the time, alone with just her thoughts.

Silk's self-love development grew in force during this five-year resurrection. It became the key to her emotional healing and well-being. Self-love starts with self-protection and Silk certainly needed to continue to protect herself during this period:

- She became increasingly aware of her core value: self-appreciation and self-respect
- She cared for her physical health by eating well, sleeping well, exercising regularly
- She protected herself from negative emotions by using her mantra
- She protected herself from the temptation to get back to the intimacy and sex with No-Name by refusing to see him (he kept coming and begging her to get back to him for almost two years after the marriage)
- She developed herself intellectually – three years after her divorce she enrolled on a PhD

Where Is She Now?

It is twenty years since Silk experienced the most profound emotional trauma of her young life. And in that time, she has become a new woman, with renewed power, energy and confidence.

- She graduated with her doctorate at the age of thirty-five.
- She continued her career path in the organisation and eventually was promoted to a Directorship.
- She fell in love with a good man – a progressive, self-aware and loving man – and married him at the age of thirty-six.
- She became a mother – she has two children at primary school.

> *"Looking back, I can see how I was lucky. Many women suffer what I suffered but many also don't move forward; they never heal. And I can understand why – it is just too painful and being women, we too easily blame ourselves for the failings of the men in our lives. I at least had a template already in my life, a good model to follow, and that was in my family and its values of honesty, incorruptibility, trust, togetherness, and non-toxicity. There was no toxic masculinity or toxic femininity in my family, not then and not now. Nor is there in my new family, my second marriage. I have let go of bitterness and anger. I have healed and I have stayed true*

182

to myself along the way. Like my family, I cannot compromise on honesty and sincerity. If I have one task left in my life, one major ambition, it is to prepare my two children for their future, guide them and instil in them the values of self-love. That is their best protection against any future trauma."

The past trauma never fully left Silk but it did transform into something positive and beautiful: her honesty, self-love and strength became prominent features of her personality, much more so than before. They came to blend with her other experiences of life to create a distinctive aura and fragrance in her heart. She has become a mature and wise shelter, guide and mentor for younger women who are going through difficult times and a great and supportive friend to all the many women who enter her orbit.

What hasn't changed is her voice, soft and low as ever; her figure, petite and small; and her appearance, so average you would pass her by without a second glance. Indeed, Silk looks like everywoman and everywoman she is. There are countless Silks among us.

But you will know if you meet a Silk because you'll not fail to feel her aura. Any pains and suffering you have will be suddenly lessened just by the warmth of this woman's eyes, by her hand touching you, or by her asking the simple question; "How are you today?". And if you were to answer in a slightly hesitant way, revealing to Silk a deeper worry or concern, she would not hurry away, disinterested. She would stay a while, talk to you and be there for you. Her friends find her the most caring and compassionate of women, always ready with a kind and supportive word, a small unexpected gift, the look of love always in her eyes.

Silk gained power from overcoming her trauma. It turned her little heart into a hub of compassion and empathy. That heart is tiny but it is strong enough to warm the whole of space.

She—
a little flower
by the country road,

with petals
violet
enough
to
turn
the whole cosmos
into
her colour.

183

Chapter Sixteen: Peace

Voice of Love Across the Universe

"OK, let's start…let me introduce myself to you.

I am a woman.

And if you ask me what is my definition of myself, of who I am, then I see myself in a variety of aspects, but basically, I am a fragile little flower and so is my heart. My heart is also very vulnerable, and sensitive and normal like anyone's heart. But within that heart is a wish. My heart wishes that it could be gigantic, athletic and strong enough to hold the whole planet earth within herself, the way a mother would hold a new-born baby within her arms.

That is how I see myself.

If you look at me from the outside then I am just like anyone. But in my inside me is a burning desire to bring love first to myself, to my surroundings and to anyone I meet. My dream is that one day the whole human race will be immersed in love. And love from the heart of the whole human race will penetrate the core of the planet earth and mingle with the love of planet earth. These two types of love will blend together and explode into the cosmos like a huge flower and the whole cosmos will welcome the arrival of mother earth. Every year that mother earth orbits around the sun then every position she comes to in space she is welcomed because she is a planet of love."

This is the story of Peace, forty-seven years on this earth and full of love for it. This Vietnamese woman overflows with love. The Vietnamese word for what is inside Binh is 'thuong', meaning love combined with compassion, respect, care and sincerity.

Peace's story is both beautiful and painful. Her life has been both easy and hard. She has grown and she has diminished. Where she is today is not where she was a decade ago. She has suffered and she has overcome.

She is a woman like all women.

Her story is hers alone but it is not unique. It is a story of one woman but it is for all women who have suffered, which means it is for every woman alive today, every woman who has ever lived, and every woman who will come to live in the future.

This is the story of Peace, forty-seven years on this earth and full of love for it. She will tell you her story in her own words.

The Beginning

I was born into the family of a Vietnamese army veteran. My father was a Vietcong guerrilla in the centre of Vietnam, an area occupied by American troops. For the love of the country he became a guerrilla. He struggled against the Americans, secretly, until his status was revealed and he had to flee his home village and into the forest where he became a Vietnamese soldier. After three years in the forest he was wounded. He lost half his right arm. He was taken to Hanoi to recover. He couldn't go back fighting so attended university and graduated as an accountant. He went to work in a factory, forty kilometres west of Hanoi, where he became the chief accountant. That is where he met my mother.

So before I was born, my father went through a lot of pain and a lot of suffering but he also had a lot of passion and courage in his heart.

My mother was the daughter of poor farmers in a province forty kilometres south of Hanoi. She married my father out of compassion and kindness more than out of love. She felt pity for the difficulties he had to go through in his daily life as an invalid from the war.

But after the marriage they had a marvellous love that lasted all their lives. My father died five years ago but he remains the biggest love of my mother's life.

So I was born into a family of kindness, sweetness, love and protection. And a lot of sympathy and understanding. My father doted on me.

My parents were not wealthy, just average people in a very poor country, a post-war country – after the war everybody was poor. But they gave me the best that they could, emotionally and materially. Never in my childhood did I experience loneliness, dissatisfaction or inferiority. Everything was rosy, everything was great, everything was sweet, everything was tender.

Also, I did very well at school.

> *Until the age of twenty-one, my life was wrapped up in success, happiness and joy, pleasure and satisfaction from all sources.*

Peace graduates from one of the leading Hanoi universities, the University of Languages and International Studies, with a degree in English literature. She is immediately appointed as a Lecturer at ULIS. With Vietnam emerging from its war trauma, millions of people are eager for a prosperous life and that means learning to speak English. Peace supplements her income by offering English classes. Life is good. She is financially independent and has a career pathway opening up before her. Then, in the third year of university, she attends a friend's birthday party and meets the man she was to marry.

Marriage

> *After we married I bought a piece of land, had a house built and went into debt. My husband had no money, no savings. His family were poor. That was the beginning of everything – all my difficulties started then. The time of plenty ended and the time of shortage in my life began. Firstly, in terms of money. And soon after the marriage, shortage came in terms of joy, kindness, sympathy and understanding.*
>
> *I found myself among in-laws who could not understand me. They were highly critical of me. What I said, what I didn't say. Even my silence upset them.*
>
> *Instinctively, I tried to create a distance between me and them.*
>
> *My husband was born in the year of the mouse, I was born in the year of the cat. And our life together was a lot like the cartoon, Tom and Jerry.*
>
> *I didn't truly love my husband for who he was, though I didn't realize that on my wedding day. I loved an image of him that I had created in my mind, and that he and his family had conspired to create for me. That image turned out to be false.*
>
> *For example, before we married he was a man with few words and a lot of silences. And I interpreted that silence as power, modesty and self-awareness. But it turned out his silence was because he didn't have anything to say! A lot of weakness hid behind that silence.*
>
> *My story is of a woman from one universe getting into another universe through marriage. But I misunderstood all of them and they misunderstood me. Two layers of misunderstanding and so*

much judgement from both sides, causing so much tension in the marriage. It killed off the love between me and him so quickly. Just one year after the birth of my son, four years after the marriage, that was it: no more love.

My story is one of a woman going through a lot of illusions; what I perceived and experienced as brutality and cruelty, both from the husband and his family. There was so much ill-will against me and I had to protect myself. I had to go through judgements, disdain and hatred – so many negative emotions towards me.

I had to learn to understand them and understand me enough so that I could see all the things I perceived as cruelty and brutality were not as I understood at the beginning. I came to understand that those people, the husband and his family, who treated me badly were also victims – of their own values and habits. And I am the victim of my own perceptions, habits and values. These layers of misunderstanding were the intellectual, psychological and mental distance between me and the husband and his family. And the journey that I went through was to bridge that distance with tolerance and compassion.

In the attempts to understand them, so I came to understand myself.

So the biggest brutality of my life, at the beginning, was the disappointment. I expected to marry into a family like my parents. And instead I found myself married into a family in which the mother was cruel to the father; brothers and sisters were judging each other and that family would judge all their in-laws. They were all cruel towards each other and I saw no love or tolerance between them. Surely, when they were that way towards each other then there was no love to me.

That disappointment brought about so much loneliness and sadness that I found myself in severe depression for twelve years.

During this twelve-year-long depression, Peace gives birth to a second child, a daughter. The child is not conceived in love and passion but in a moment when she mistakenly believes her husband when he claims to have changed, when he says he understands Peace and her trauma with him and his family and wants to make amends. He is all sweetness and light towards Peace. He momentarily acts in a loving, compassionate and emotionally intelligent way and Peace wants to believe him. But as she was to discover, it is all just another illusion.

The Depths

During these twelve years I was very frustrated with all my life. I felt helpless. Physically, I could not take proper care of myself, let alone do anything to change my life. But the worst thing of all is that for the first seven years of those depression years I did not know that it was depression. I did not know that it was an emotional illness. I thought I had a disease. I just tried to survive each day. Every day was darkness. Every day was coldness. Every day was helplessness. Every day was bad.

I was exhausted with looking after my young children, being a housewife and working full-time. I could barely look after myself. I lost weight. I wasn't eating properly. I was like a zombie, just going through a routine without knowing what or why. I was just trying to survive each day. I had no hope, no expectations, no happiness and no release from the deep emptiness within me. I was slowly dying inside.

There was one morning, I think it was the worst morning, I woke up, opened my eyes and I looked around the room and I asked myself '----, do you want to continue to live in this life?' Give me one reason to continue to live this life. What is the point? Nothing is interesting. Nothing is good. Nothing is attractive enough for me to go on living. And I thought of the Korean singer, aged twenty-seven, who committed suicide the day before. I was in complete sympathy with her. That morning, my muscles would not allow me to sit up. I felt like I was a piece of paper – helpless, stuck to the mattress of the bed. I lay there for, I think, thirty minutes. Then suddenly, the face of my mother came into my head. The way she looked at me startled me. I asked myself how could I betray the love and care my parents gave me and die in this way?

I asked myself what is the cause of my pain, my feeling of wanting to die? And the answer that came was my in-laws and my husband. And the life I had. It was too bad.

That life was not worth living. The next question that came into my head was 'how can you allow those people to harm the happiness of your mother and your father? Because if you die they will be the ones to suffer.'

Then I began to find strength inside me. For the first time I realised it was not only me as an individual: I was the continuation of my mother and my father. I realised that by letting these people harm me I was allowing them to harm my parents, all my ancestors and everything they symbolised. Suddenly, I found a lot of energy in me. Then I began to take action.

I looked at my left hand and I told myself it was the embodiment of my parents. My right hand was me. I held my hands together and promised myself that on behalf of the whole world I would protect you, take care of you, not let anyone harm you, disrespect you or treat you badly because you are worthy of all the best in the world. For you I will fight. For you I will do anything I need to do.

From that moment on I started to change.

The Rising Up

How did I change? I stopped internalising people's judgements, negative comments and hostility, and I stopped reacting to them the way I used to. Let me give you an example...when I was small I was very obedient and whenever my parents told me that my behaviour was bad it meant it was bad and I tried to change my behaviour because I took their comments literally. But when my mother-in-law told me my behaviour was bad it didn't mean my behaviour was bad but that she wanted me to feel bad about myself. What was bad from her perspective does not mean something was bad. So if I took her words literally as I did my parent's words, I would kill myself. I would be cruel to myself. In that way I would be assisting them to harm myself. So the first change I did was to stop internalising people's attitudes and behaviour towards me. I came to realise that I needed to filter everything I got from the outside through love, care and protection, so toxicity would not take root in my inner self.

It took me a lot of time and energy to do that. To set up a new habit is not easy. Sometimes you make a mistake, you forget and you get hurt. But whenever I made a mistake I would review it from the beginning.

My life was like a battlefield at that time.

But I would not argue with those who attacked me, I would not attack them back. I would not knock them, or look down on them. I would not judge them. I would stop all that but at the same time I would start to say good, kind and positive words to myself, as self-protection and self-healing only.

And after a while, the depression is gone.

As this process was going on within me I also got assistance from a doctor. This doctor helped me unconditionally. I met her in my evening classes when I was teaching English. She spent a lot of time taking care of me, telling me my depression was not because of some physical reason in my system – there was nothing wrong with me. It was just the external circumstances that caused me stress.

She helped find me a good doctor who prescribed some medicine for my stress. Then she helped me take care of my physical health when I reduced my medication. After six months I reduced the medication. But then the stress came back after three months. So I took another six months of medication then reduced it. Again the stress came back. I then took a further six months of full dosage medication and began to reduce the dosage. But three months later the stress was gradually coming back. On that particular day I took the decision that I would have to take the medicine all my life, no matter what the side-effects would be. It was impossible for me to live without medicine.

Then a friend took me to a Pagoda where I spent two days and nights meditating. By the second day the kind of chemical that is supposed to be provided by the medicine was full inside me. My body was thriving. All signs of exhaustion and stress were gone. After just two days of meditating regularly I was changed.

I recognised that if I meditated I would not have to take the medicine. Some corner of my brain would produce that chemical when I meditated.

That was the beginning of a new and more hopeful, healthier, phase of my life. I started doing meditation like a hobby, like a treatment, as a time that I reserved for myself. Like an oasis of peace in a world of chaos, brutality and darkness, loneliness, suffering and hardship.

It was that way for over a year.

Peace has finally found peace within herself through meditation and through applying those principles of self-love that were to become a central aspect of her character and identity as a woman. She is learning to let go of suffering by embracing it as a vehicle for her self-improvement as a human. She is learning to let go of anger by recognising it is a powerful element of her self but also a dangerous one which needs to be monitored, controlled, not allowed to run amok within her consciousness. And she is letting go of bitterness for those who have caused her pain by understanding them as victims of their own years of suffering – they too have been where she is but have not been able to emerge to a better place.

The rising up of Peace through self-awareness and meditative practice signals the end of the third phase in her life, the phase of emerging from depression, suicidal thoughts and deep despair. But the suffering is not yet over. After a year of meditative practice, a new, even deeper darkness descends on Peace.

A New Darkness

My life slowly improved throughout the first year of my meditative practice, until the day I discovered my husband had another woman. It was like a bomb in my heart. I knew that I did not love him and I was not jealous of him or the other woman, I even felt happy for him because he had love in his life. All his life he had never had happiness in love. The pain that I had was trust being betrayed. I had invested all of myself into that marriage. The core value that I had was that if you treated people well you would be treated well in return.

I had gone into my marriage with that value imprinted in my heart, from my parents. But all I had received from my husband and his family was the very opposite of what I gave them.

I asked myself was I too stupid or were they too bad?

Losing him to another woman did not bring me pain. What brought me pain was the collapse of my core values. It was the pain of seeing that the value I had for life was not realistic. All the attempts to live in the way I used to live had brought me to this moment. I witnessed at that time all my dedication, honesty and effort I had put into the marriage were returned to me with bitterness, dishonesty and frustration. I found myself down in the bottom of the pain, and the pain came in waves.

For the first two weeks after finding out about the affair I was completely normal. I behaved exactly as the self-help books on marriage advise you to. You should forgive him, you should give him the chance to come back, you should treat him with respect, this and that. I could do all that so well because I was not jealous. But gradually, the inner things began to reveal themselves.

About three weeks after the discovery of the affair the pain rushed in and it was unimaginable. I lost 7 kg in three months. I

191

could not eat. There was no light in my eyes. My breasts became exceptionally flat. My skin was pale.

For the first time in my life I realized that emotional pain can turn into physical pain. It was a terrible pain in my heart, in my gut, in my muscles. Some mornings I woke up feeling like I had a two huge snakes fighting each other in my gut. I was exhausted.

I asked myself over and over again, how could you be so silly? And some days I would answer with optimism, telling myself that I could change my life for the better. These were the rational days.

But the next day would be a pain-filled day. It totally enveloped me.

Each day the pain would be different. For example, one day I might wake up and find my gut is fine today, there are no snakes fighting in my gut. But instead I find a small dot in my heart, like a needle. And I told myself – okay Peace you have a lucky day today, you will not be killed by the pain. It has reduced. But the needle in my heart would grow during the day and at the end of it I was exhausted like the previous day.

It rotated in this way: a day of deadly emotional pain, followed by a day of very positive rational thinking. And so it went on and on, in waves through me. But the phases gradually got longer and longer, slowly reducing and weakening. Until three years later they were all gone.

Peace has reached the age of thirty-eight. She has been married for fifteen years, has two young children and her own home. She has a career in academia, loving parents, but a failed marriage and an unfaithful husband who is himself the product of a family diseased by toxicity, both female and male.

It is out of this reality that she must now forge her new self.

The New Peace

Three years after that incident I was a totally new woman. I could recall events but without the surges of pain. How did this come about? I was meditating every day but also I was reconceptualising things in my life.

Meditating only could help me to get rid of the emotions and thoughts for a while, but when I ended the meditation phase the harsh reality would come back. So over those three years I did meditation but I also did one more thing, I shifted my values, I shifted my daily habits. Also those were the years when I went through the layers of misunderstanding between me and my husband and my in-laws. I could see them from the inside out, from their own perspective. I began to discern the difference between me and them. I began to find out why they had interpreted me so wrongly at the beginning; why they could not understand me nor me them. I realised that the me they see is totally different from the me in my eyes. I recognised that even though we were sharing the same house, the same meals, and the same life, my world was very different to how they lived in their world. That was when I knew there could never be a realignment of love and understanding.

So I had to reconstruct their image in my heart.

At first I thought they were cruel. Now I only thought that they were ignorant.

At first I thought that they were greedy. Now I only thought that they were needy.

At first I thought that they were very unfaithful. Now I only thought that they were only faithful to themselves.

In fact, during those years my negative judgement for those people did reduce a lot. In other words, it was during those three years of darkness in my life that I got rid of the darkness in my life. I had to face the darkness for my own life. I started to cast light into the darkness and by the end of those three years I could recall the bad emotions without feeling those bad emotions. The wisdom of understanding dispersed the illusions of misunderstanding and discern the differences.

Without the darkness of those negative forces my life quality was so much better.

It was at this time I started to find peace in me.

The stress disappeared. My life came back to me.

And if you were to ask me what is the best medication for stress I would say it is the trauma.

I took medication prescribed by the doctors. And I did meditation. But both the medication and the meditation helped me improve my mindset only a little bit. Not enough to bring me to peace and joy, fun and excitement. So I could survive stress with medication and meditation but I could not thrive, I could not fully live.

It was the trauma which forced me to reconceptualise the reality.

It was the trauma that forced me to think again, look again, to question everything around me and inside me, that brought me out of the confusion and out of the pain.

During those days, the vigorous attempts I made to save me from the pain became more and more powerful each day. By the time the depression was over, that momentum helped me to rise to another higher frequency. That was the frequency of joy.

Before that, joy was a frequency I would achieve when something good happened. But by the end of that phrase, joy was a frequency when nothing bad happened.

Joy became the home frequency of myself.

And Onward in Love

Today, Peace lives in harmony with her everyday joy. She sees beauty in the most ordinary things. She will stop during a walk in the park, stoop down and take a photo of a tiny, innocuous flower hiding in the bushes. She will be in a restaurant looking out on the busy street and see the strength and fortitude of the old gnarled tree by the roadside. She will inhale the air and sense love and goodness in it. She will see her Sacred U in the clouds.

And she will look at you and see your depths, your aura. She can look into your heart and understand you, better perhaps than you can understand yourself. She can hear your words before you have spoken them.

That is because Peace is an empath.

One day I read an article posted on the internet about empaths. I read that article out of curiosity and I was shocked because but it answered so many questions in me.

For example, why am I so sensitive? When I was twenty my friends told me I was over-sensitive. And I thought, what is wrong with being over-sensitive? And people told me that if I was over-sensitive then I could maximise everything; small things can be seen as huge. Then I would not be able to survive in life.

The usual way of surviving in life is when you have a problem, a big problem, you must try and view the problem in a way that it becomes diminished to a smaller scale and a small problem can be further diminished into nothing. But with being sensitive, like me, small things become maximised, and big things become overwhelming.

Being that sensitive is a curse because I sense everything. Down to the tiny little bit. Many other women I know had their husband betray them but for them it was not so terrible. They could go on and live with their husband. But I could not.

Other people go through the loss of trust and faith, or had to reshape their values in life, but their pain seems so much less. So why for me was it so bad?

For many years I thought it was a weakness because I had too much kindness, love and care in me and I was not vaccinated against the sufferings of life. I looked at myself as an unvaccinated person. I was even envious of those who had less sensitivity – who, when they were abused, were mistreated or suffered from some minor trauma, they then developed their own immune system so they became strong. They were able to survive the traumas of life.

But when I read the article about the empath I realised it was not necessarily a weakness I had. Instead, I had to learn to deal with things in a more in-depth, minute way; that way I could find a solution to my problem or trauma. For the same trauma in another person it would take them just one tenth of the energy I needed to put in so as to overcome the feelings within me. So for me, it was ten times worse than for a normal person.

My friends used to joke about me. They called me the 'Dr of Suffering' because I did so much pondering and thinking about suffering. I could categorise suffering into different types, and these types I sub-categorised into smaller types and in these smaller types I could describe their individual nuances in minute detail.

But my friends enjoyed talking to me because when they had a problem they could see the problem only vaguely but when they talked to me I could analyse the shapes and the nuances of their suffering. And after talking to me they had a better insight into their own problem. The negative feelings attached to the problem were lessened.

And so I started to gather around me the people who are going through traumas and problems because when they looked at me they saw someone who suffered more than them. So they were assured that I would not judge them for being a failure in life because I was even worse. When they talked to me they had someone who could understand all of their sufferings so well even more than they could understand themselves.

My friends found a joy in talking to me about their problems because I had gone through my own sufferings and eventually had found joy unconditionally.

I realised I had no single reason to be lonely at all because I was surrounded by so much love and appreciation from people.

Within my husband's family there was no more hatred or disdain or anything. I did not go to the extreme of trying to be close to my in-laws, trying to be intimate with them or trying to be one with them, but I was totally free from hatred or judgement towards them.

I could be very honest with my love and I could be very honest with my hatred. I began to realise the state of being at ease and happy in hatred. I don't judge myself at all, for anything.

For example, people may think that to truly love someone is to forgive them. But I don't have to force myself in that way. I firstly have to forgive myself. So if one day I hate a person then I have to first forgive myself for hating that person. I would ask myself why I hate that person. I would analyse my hatred for that person and I would understand it. But my hatred for that person is embraced in my own love for it. And after a while, the love overwhelms the hatred. There is no more hatred.

The hatred is a like a baby. It is fed with love, it then begins to sleep. I see beauty in hatred but it is in my heart. I don't look at the person with hatred, or act in hatred, or do anything in hatred. I just am honest with my hatred.

I found further traits in me with are typical of an empath. And I began to fall in love with myself more and more each day.

I found myself more beautiful each day. I found myself surrounded by more love and trust each day. I could not find any sign of suffering or loneliness within me. I found a lot of beauty in my heart.

On the days she is joyful and happy, full of love, my heart is beautiful and I admire her.

But on the days she is frustrated, angry, contemptuous, I find she is beautiful too.

Just like when you are by the sea and the sea is calm, you can swim in the sea and you can enjoy the calm sea.

But on the days you are at the sea and it is a stormy day you don't swim in the sea but you can still see the beauty of the sea, the joy in the storms, the wind, the clouds, pushing the water into huge waves. So violent but also so beautiful.

So there are many nuances of beauty.

Nothing is ugly in nature.

The monsoon is beautiful in its own way.
The breeze is beautiful in its own way.
The darkness is beautiful in its own way.
And the sunlight is surely beautiful in its own way.

And so is my heart.

And gradually I came to realise that the things which happen in my heart are at the same nature with what happens out there, in the world around me, in the nature. Sometimes there is a storm, sometimes a breeze.

A storm can surge up in Hanoi after a butterfly fluttering around a flower in the Amazon river. If some day there is a storm in my heart. Its not my job to say whether the storm should stay or go. It's not my job to say there should be or not be a storm. The only thing that I should do is to embrace my heart no matter how it is. The way I would embrace the nature.

So I respect myself the way I respect the nature. So I begin to treasure myself the way I treasure the nature.

And I realise that everyone's heart is of the same nature.

You don't need to travel to a tourist spot to get in touch with nature.

You don't need to be by the ocean to witness the vastness of the nature.

Just look at your heart.

You will find the most beautiful things and the most amazing things, there.

I have found that my heart is the part of the most natural flow of life. My body is a part of the natural flow of life. And each day I open my eyes I just welcome the flow of life in me the way it is, without trying to change it at all.

Enjoy every day the way it is.

And I suddenly realised I no more judge people the way they are. If they are stupid it is because the power of stupidity is dancing and dominating within them. It is not my job to say that they should be wise. It is not my job to say that they should be different. And it is not their job to do anything about that.

The only thing that we should do in this life is to be admiring and embracing everything with love.

When you choose not to be against anything, when you choose to embrace everything with love, suddenly nothing comes but love.

I began to realise that I got richer and richer every day in terms of emotion. Life got better, and better. Experience has taught me that even if something bad happened to me, sooner or later it will turn into something good. So long as I have the patience to embrace everything that is not yet good for my life. Because I have learned that the nature of life is so good that everything improves. Everyone improves as the time goes by.

One day I realised that 'growth mindset' has replaced the 'static mindset' in me. And while I embrace that growth mindset, nothing needs improving. Nothing needs changing. And yet everything naturally improves.

And then wonders started to unfold.

One evening I was walking in the park and I looked up to the sky and saw a star twinkling and suddenly there seems to be a word of love to me from the star. The other day I was walking in the park and a breeze was blowing and suddenly I realised in that breeze there is a voice of love whispering to me.

So I see love in everything that happens to me.

In the morning or afternoon I see the grey mists of the horizon and I see love for me in that mist. I see love for me in the sky, I see love for me whenever my feet touch the ground; love from the earth, the sky, the plants and a lot of love from the people I meet.

I found that love can come in so many ways.

Every day I talk to that someone who has created all this, I call it Sacred U. I tell them I admire them so much, I admire their magic, their beauty, their love so much that I never want to die, I want to live as long as I can.

I tell them I want to learn all your wisdom, all your magic, and I say that if the way you teach me is through trauma then I want to go through all the trauma that you have in store for me.

I am not afraid of anything because I know that ultimately there is always love for me at the end of the road.

I started to find in me so much love for the wholeness and wholesomeness of life and in the sacred nature of life. I started to develop the habit of talking to that wholeness every day, expressing my love for that wholeness every day. I found in my heart so much love for that wholeness to the level that sometimes I wanted to scream so loud that my voice would go to the very outer rim of this universe. I want to let the whole universe know that I love her. I love everything that is in existence. I want to shout so long so that my words of love for this universe would echo from the beginning to the end of the timeline of the universe.

So after this life, if there is a later life and if I am born again, the first sound that I would hear from life is the echo from the sound of love that I have made in this life.

I believe that echo will be kept in the memory of the universe; it will be kept in the soil, in the air, in the leaves, in the tree trunks, and that echo would come back to me. Reminding me of the beautiful nature, the sacred nature of love and of life.

That is what my life is like now.

Part Three: Cure

Chapter Seventeen: Achieving Independence Through Totally Inclusive Self-Love

It is likely we are born with self-love. It is not so likely we will die with it. In between, life takes its toll on us. And we take a toll on ourselves.

The twelve women portrayed in this book were never entirely innocent victims. They made some bad decisions. They often acted badly towards others, including their husbands. And they hung on to myths and illusions, both about themselves and their partners. When confronted with harsh reality they often chose to look away, to go on pretending. Until the day came when they had to stop pretending – when it was clearly in their best interests to ditch whatever innocence or ignorance they had left.

In other words, these twelve women acted in ways that are entirely human. No one reading this book can claim to be any different to these twelve women. None of us can claim to be entirely innocent, entirely devoid of toxicity and entirely open to reality. The only certain angels are those in our imagination. Only the very young can justly claim to be innocent. The rest of us, certainly all adults, are forever swinging between goodness and toxicity, charity and meanness, generosity and self-centeredness, need and greed, stupidity and insight.

There may not be any single answer to any of these dilemmas. Indeed, it is reasonable to expect humans to go on making the same mistakes, acting in the same toxic stupid manner, as they have down the ages. In which case, not much changes. It may even get worse. AI is becoming a clear competitor to human intelligence – indeed, it could result in the diminishment of human intelligence. How can you be sure some AI device has not written this book? Well, for one thing, it is unlikely that AI or any of its offspring are going to be heavily into emotional intelligence and certainly not self-love.

If you wish to distinguish a human reaction from an AI reaction, look for the tears – and the suffering behind them.

And there is an ocean of tears and suffering in this book. It was emotional for us to know these women, learn their stories and write those stories for you. And it is undoubtedly emotional to be one of these women. In truth, it is emotional to be any woman, anywhere.

If humanity is to have a future it lies not with more technology but with more self-love; in which case, developing the emotional intelligence and practices to engender self-awareness, self-validation, empathy and self-management is now our most urgent priority.

Humanity can save itself through love. There seems to us no healthy alternative. And that love must start within us.

If we want a better world then simply hoping for it won't get you very far. Nor will despairing of ever achieving it. We have to have hope and that hope must start with ourselves, within our selves. Every individual who loves themselves in a healthy, positive, sustainable way makes the most important and positive contribution to the whole of humanity. Because if you love yourself then you will be kind and understanding to yourself and therefore much more likely to be kind understanding towards others.

That is Totally Inclusive Self-Love.

The impact of self-love cannot be overstated. It is not simply an agent of change, it is a detoxifier. Self-love detoxifies the whole person – body, mind and soul.

Imagine eight billion detoxified humans. We'd have a very different world and be facing a very different future.

Sure, unrealistic, you will say. If need and desire for self-love is innate in humans, then so is envy, insecurity, competitiveness, jealousy, greed, and the biggest toxic-generator of all – fear.

Fear is the devil in the detail in the stories of these twelve women. It is usually unacknowledged but always present; constantly hovering in the background like a chilling wraith. In truth, we all have fear in us – we are all having to live with it. And most of us don't live with it very well.

- We fear never loving or being loved

- We fear losing love

- We fear never having what we desire, need or want,

- We fear losing what we have acquired

- We fear becoming irrelevant

- We fear what happens next

- We fear what happens at the end

A lot of fear and very little comfort.

Predictably, we respond to such existential insecurity by surrounding ourselves with myths – fairy tales, fables and fictions designed to assuage our fear while providing us with garments with which to clothe our naked self. And why not? After all, they are readily available to us: handed down generation after generation and reinforced by family, friends and society – the myths of toxic femininity, for example. These myths don't require us to question they don't really want us to think too much, we merely need to assimilate the myths and believe them. And to reinforce those myths, or at least to stop us thinking too critically about them, we retreat to comfort zones; conspicuous consumption, sex, alcohol, drugs – whatever distractions occupy one's mind, momentarily take our attention away from the existential issues lurking in our thoughts and our imagination.

The twelve women in this book have all suffered from fear, anxiety and insecurity and none have fully eradicated these elements from their lives. Not even the four women who have acquired various levels of self-love – Alchemist, Heart, Silk and Peace – can claim to be totally without fear in their lives. But what they have acquired is a greater tranquillity. They have become more content and moments of happiness and joy are increased in frequency for each of them. Fear in them is not a prevailing emotion. It has been marginalised, to the benefit of their emotional and physical wellbeing.

Who wouldn't want to be in a state of mindful joy, contentment and self-appreciation, freed from the nagging noise of fear and anxiety?

If we can learn from the experiences of others then it saves a lot of time and a lot of anguish. And we can learn from these women.

What Can We Learn from the Twelve?

Probably the single most important lesson is that independence does not come easy for any female no matter her background and intersectional identity. Independent femininity has to be worked at and it has to be achieved, which means having many battles not least within oneself. It means actively rejecting the myths of toxic femininity because no woman can become independent in mind and body until she rejects those myths designed to control her, restrict her opportunities, dictate who and what she can be. A woman may well get help in identifying the myths of toxic femininity, indeed that the aim of this book, but only she can release herself from the grip of these myths – no one can or will bequeath independence to any woman. Independence has to be attained – just like self-love. Inevitably, only the woman herself can become independent; because first and foremost it is a state of mind not simply a state of material wealth, class or education.

Each of the twelve women in this book have had their battles but the biggest one has been convincing themselves that they were worthy of independence. This is the hardest battle facing every female because to win it they must reject the dominant narrative informing gender identity – which is that men provide the protection and support, women flourish under that protective masculinity. This message still gets pushed out to women around the world with many men actively promoting such propaganda: the traditionalists, the misogynists and all those troubled men who judge 'independent woman' to be the ultimate oxymoron if not a personal threat.

This tells us that the first step towards independent femininity is for the female to recognise and accept what she is stepping away from – and that stepping away requires self-awareness and self-appreciation. She must distinguish between, for example, lust and love; wanting and needing; cooperation and compliance; effort and sacrifice; silence and fear. She must not be ashamed of her identity, her sexuality, her desires, her weaknesses, her body or her inconsistences. She must privilege and protect her independent mindset, agency and authenticity and not be tempted to sell these cheap in order to meet the expectations of others. She must recognise that desiring intimacy with a man is not the same as wanting to be controlled by him – she has every right to seek the former without ever having to compromise on the latter. And she must not carry a baggage of guilt and regret every time her efforts at independence falter in the face of social pressure.

Independent femininity will look different with every woman, but what is common amongst all is that it is independence from men: from relying exclusively and solely on men, from seeking validation from men and from believing their worth is only ever a condition of the male gaze and men's judgements.

Some of the twelve women had the odds stacked against them from the outset, others were more advantaged in their upbringing and family circumstances. But not one of these twelve could take anything for granted; even when life appeared to be smooth and carefree there were always crises and challenges lurking around the next corner. But whatever life threw at them if they were to achieve independence then they had to persist, they could never give up.

A further lesson is that achieving independent femininity does not demand a woman live a solo life, free of any deep emotional attachment to a man. <u>Divorce, separation, solo-living and childlessness are not prerequisites of independent femininity</u>. Though it does appear that increasing numbers of women believe otherwise and are structuring their lives accordingly. We see this as simply women taking a hard look at the options around them and deciding, logically and rationally, to reject traditional gender roles and narratives in favour of independent femininity.

This is feminine agency in action and no society can or should ignore it. Nor should any man.

These twelve stories show that there is no innocent, unadulterated woman. There is no pure femininity as opposed to a toxic femininity. But there is a femininity that is healthier and far more positive than the toxic version. There is a way of being a woman that is more likely to engender peace, contentment, laughter and joy and the only way that can be achieved for any woman is through activating whatever agency she might have.

In other words, envisaging, creating, designing and pursuing an independent femininity while recognising it to be her own, and every other woman's, birthright.

Inside every woman, every human, there exists both light and dark; good and bad. The aim, therefore, must be to turn oneself into more light than dark. We may never be able to fully eradicate darkness but maybe we don't need to.

Because without darkness there is no light. Without evil there is no good. Pain is vital – it signals that something is amiss in our bodies or our minds. We live in a world of inevitable binaries. Each binary is self-sustaining. We need to recognise toxicity in order to appreciate goodness and kindness. We need to acknowledge the dark in each of us so as to enhance the light in each of us. We need to know when we are being toxic so we know when we are being empathic, good, understanding, generous, patient, warm and enabling.

The twelve women in our book will never be free of these struggles. But then, neither are you, neither are any of us. That is one of the conditions of life – to struggle and hopefully to learn from those struggles. Even if we cannot fully overcome, we can always learn, we can always grow, we can always become better versions of ourselves.

We can see both similarities and differences in the lives of these twelve women – each is a unique individual with her own life story, history, mix of competing pressures and intersectional identity. What we can learn from this is to appreciate and value our uniqueness while also working to recognise and understand what constitutes that uniqueness.

A useful exercise, therefore, is to list the components, the elements and factors that constitute who you are. What does your intersectionality look like and which of these elements are you in control of and which not? Which are you valuing and which not? Which do you want to change and which are you content to leave untouched?

This is not just a mental exercise, it is a good way to delve deeper into your own identity constructs while recognising some of the forces which combine and conspire to create your unique individuality – your self.

Having named, listed and accepted your intersectionalized self you are then in a better position to proceed to the next step – which is to love it.

If you yearn and strive for an independent femininity then do so first from a place of self-recognition and self-awareness. This is the garden within which your self-love with grow.

But perhaps the most important lesson these twelve women give us is never to stop, never to give up, never to quit and never to succumb to toxicity. Because life can get better: it will get better – you will emerge from the darkness eventually. So long as you keep on the path.

And a key step on the path to self-love concerns the biggest single obstacle to self-love – suffering.

Learning from Suffering

Suffering gets a bad name. Who among us would vote for more suffering? Who among us would opt for suffering when pleasure is available? Who wants more suffering, not less, in their lives?

But suffering is like illness – you will not live without it. It will find you no matter where you hide, no matter how robust you imagine you are.

In this case, maybe we can turn suffering into something positive? Because for sure, that is what most of the twelve women have done, even if they don't necessarily realise it.

Taking a debit and credit approach to suffering, what is on the debit side? The negatives to suffering are easy to note;

- sadness, disappointment

- regret, shame, guilt

- stress, anxiety, insecurity

- a sense of inferiority

- a sense of hopelessness

- a sense of failure

Bad enough, but it doesn't end there, because resentment of these emotions and their causes leads to a deeper layer of suffering – when our physical and mental health starts to decline to dangerous levels. Then we are into the depression levels experienced by, for example, Peace (her depression lasted over a decade). That is when the suicidal thoughts start to peek through into our consciousness.

Yet how often in life is it that we turn the corner only after reaching the end? In other words, as with Peace, it was the depression that eventually triggered in her the desire to improve her life, to get better. So it was with most of our twelve women – they reached rock bottom and then started to rise up.

The most difficult step in the awakening, healing, self-love journey is the first one. Because that is when we need to find the energy, motivation and resolve to kick-start the necessary pro-active shift in our mindset. Suffering at least provides us with that possibility, that motivation – that kick in the butt. Indeed, failure and suffering provide us with a wealth of benefits.

On the credit side…

Experiencing suffering can make a person;

- more empathetic, sensitive to the same sufferings in other individuals

- more likely to be compassionate to those who suffer similarly

- more likely to want to protect others from suffering

- less likely to be egotistical, arrogant, entitled

These are all beautiful, precious facets in a person. But they don't always come naturally or automatically. Empathy needs to be worked at, for example. Compassion is always up against self-interest. And those who never suffer, never have hardship, may enjoy a good life on the outside but inside they are less likely to be wise, self-aware and knowing. Suffering is a source of anguish but also a source of beauty – if we allow it to be.

Beauty comes in many forms and one of them is self-awareness; understanding our selves through suffering and hardship

- recognising our strengths and weaknesses

- seeing patterns within our responses to suffering

- understanding the impact of suffering on our mental and physical health and wellbeing

- identifying the causes of the suffering

- developing resolve and determination to change our circumstances, our lives

- becoming courageous, strong, brave

Suffering can be a source of strength and understanding. It can be our ally, our enabler, not our destroyer – if we allow it to be.

So how can a suffering woman turn the hopelessness into hope?

- Embrace her self and her current sufferings and pains the way she might embrace her own babies: with love, tolerance, care and protection.

- Allow herself to cry, to express her pains and sufferings.

- Allow herself to be weak, to feel low, to be exhausted or demotivated…. (accept herself as she is).

- Observe her pains and sufferings the way she would observe her beloved babies: discern their peculiarities, their surging patterns and how they push her into actions and words.

- Set up compassionate connections with her sufferings and pains, allowing them to be themselves, and simultaneously acknowledge that the actual decision maker is she herself, not the pain => dis-identify with the pain, set up her agency towards the pain and manage her behaviour and words.

- Analyse various nuances of the same pain/ suffering in various circumstances, towards various people so as to identify the values/ tendencies/ patterns that lie deep in her core. Removing or shifting them will allow the pain/suffering to ease and gradually stop surging up.

- Compare herself each day with the day before, to see how dealing with sufferings turns her into a better version => treasure the positive impact of suffering on her development, see the momentum of development and maintain a realistic optimism about herself and her future.

- Acknowledge her own beauty, setting up the habit of seeing herself through her own dimensions/ norms so as to appreciate herself properly.

Turning suffering into hope, beauty, wellbeing and empowerment may seem the most unlikely of counter-intuitive possibilities. But it does work. Several of the women in our book prove it. If it works for them, then it can work for you. Sure, it won't happen overnight. But what can happen overnight is your decision to begin the process. That is an immediate step forward and once started the benefits to you will grow in profusion.

Our Twelve Women

Each of our twelve women, with her imperfectness and sufferings, is beautiful. That beauty is constantly changing, for the better. Each of them has a gem at her core; each of them is evolving into the masterpiece they were meant to be. And we writers have had the privilege of seeing them as the raw, unfinished piece. We have been privileged to be told their stories, and to have been touched by their inner beauty. We hope you are touched by it too.

So where are they now?

Ten of the twelve women in this book currently exist at different stages or dimensions of the self-love continuum outlined in the Introduction to this book:

1. Self-awareness

2. Self-validation combined with self-expression

3. Self-care combined with self-protection

4. Self-sufficiency combined self-independence

5. Self-management combined with self-development

Two women, Void and Lost, have not reached self-awareness; they have not yet begun their self-love journey and maybe never will. One reason for this could be that as mother and daughter they sustain and reinforce each other's life view, which draws heavily on toxic femininity, via their family culture. But even with Void and Lost, there is the potential for change so long as the circumstances are right, the moment is right, and they can come to believe in themselves.

Six of the ten, the battling women (Shame, Courage, Poet, Princess, Flower and Bird), are currently in the very midst of their fight for self-validation, self-independence and a better life. They are moving on from self-awareness and are battling towards Totally Inclusive Self-Love. For some of them, that battle now involves divorce; for others it is a battle against their inner demons, their desires, their weaknesses and their illusions. But each of them has strengths and each of them has hope. They will all get there eventually – with or without the love of a man to provide them with external physical and emotional comfort – because they know the price of failure. They have personal experience of it.

The four women with self-love – Alchemist, Heart, Silk and Peace – are in a better place, though not the same place. They each have challenges ahead;

the risk of feeling superior to other women precisely because they love themselves so much; the risk of allowing their feeling of security to make them complacent; and the risk of one day allowing old demons to resurface. But the signs are very positive for them. Alchemist, Heart and Silk, have already begun to emulate Peace by providing support and guidance to other women suffering from toxic femininity and broken relationships.

And that is a very important outcome of self-love in women – they can cascade goodness, wisdom, support, empathy, understanding and awareness to other women trapped in similarly damaging and toxic situations.

Change is never confined to the single individual – its flows out to others and gets reconstituted in others through ideas, behaviours and values. Women with Totally Inclusive Self-Love are the most positive role model for girls and young women that it is possible to have. Recognising this, it makes it all the more crucial that the change we create is positive not negative. There is already enough negativity, anxiety, hatred, toxicity – and fear, in the world today.

Totally Inclusive Self-love is the only answer, the only response which will work. Feeding hatred and abuse with more hatred and abuse just creates a torrent of hatred and abuse which we all have to experience and endure.

It all just magnifies the suffering of humanity.

Our twelve women provide a snapshot of the reality experienced by women around the world. It is only a snapshot but it is revealing. It tells us much about the condition of women at this point in the twenty-first century, and the condition of men. These twelve stories are salutary and disturbing but also filled with hope, wisdom and insight. The women in these stories are real but ordinary – and all the more potent and powerful for being real and ordinary. We are well aware that there are countless numbers of women around the world suffering even more harshly from toxic femininity and the gendered conditioning and conditions which sustain it.

In her own way, each woman in our book is an icon. Each woman should be recognised and respected for what she has undergone and for what she has overcome. Each woman should be acknowledged for being a survivor; a gladiator in the arena of life continuing to stand up and fight even after receiving potentially fatal blows to her self-esteem and self-confidence.

All these women have loved men. They have all wanted men in their lives; as fathers, lovers, husbands, mentors or friends. Too often, those relationships failed – leaving the woman floundering, lost, confused, angry and distraught – in some instances brutalised. Every one of them ended up disappointed and disenchanted. They joined the mass ranks of women disappointed in love and disenchanted with men.

We have to ask ourselves whether the disappointment and disenchantment of women with men is a natural condition of the sexes or something that can be changed for the better. We hope the latter. Indeed, this book is written with that hope in mind. Though right now all the evidence points to women and men growing further apart rather than becoming closer.

We have deliberately avoided discussing toxic masculinity in any depth as this topic is fully explored in many other books recently published, including one by Stephen. This is not to say toxic masculinity is unimportant in the lives of these women – and all women. Just the opposite – it is central to the lived experiences of women everywhere.

And yes, we can provide you with any number of valid reasons, supported by an overwhelming evidential base, to show why men need to change – ideally by grasping the self-love opportunities open to women.

But let us not wait for that change to happen. Women cannot wait for the majority of men to become less toxic, for gender ideologies and stereotypes to disappear and for gender and sexual conventions to be eradicated, but they can do something about their own lives and about their own femininity. Each woman can take action to begin and progress her journey to independent femininity nourished by a self-love that is totally inclusive, that marginalises no one, that embraces diversity and that is not validated by others, but that recognises we each exist because we all exist. Nothing is more likely to change the world, to make it a better place for all, than having women reject toxic femininity (and by implication, toxic masculinity) and embark on their individual walk to enlightenment, joy, contentment, happiness, self-fulfillment, peace and independence.

Happiness is finding the Harbour of Peace after countless days searching.

Happiness is recognising that the Harbour of
Peace is right there, within your chest.

Happiness is realising that no matter how far you wander into life's
tornados, you have never truly been away from that Harbour of Peace.

Related Titles from Stephen Whitehead

On Women

Van, T. Binh, and Whitehead, S. (2024) *Self-Love for Women: Overcoming Toxic Femininity and Suffering.* Luton, UK: Acorn Books.

Whitehead, S. (2024) Toxic Femininity/Hegemonic Femininity: Patriarchal-defined gender identity association in https://independent.academia.edu/StephenWhitehead6.

On Men

Whitehead, S. (1999) Hegemonic Masculinity Revisited in https://www.academia.edu/78712410/Hegemonic_Masculinity_Revisited.

Whitehead, S. and Barrett, F. (2002) *The Masculinities Reader:* Cambridge: Polity.

Whitehead, S. (2002) *Men and Masculinities.* Cambridge: Polity.

Whitehead, S. (2004) *The Many Faces of Men.* London: Arrow.

Whitehead, S. (2021) *Toxic Masculinity: Curing the Virus. Making men smarter, healthier, safer.* Luton, UK: Acorn Books.

On Total Inclusivity

Aow, A., Hollins. S. and Whitehead, S. (2022) *Becoming a Totally Inclusive School.* London: Routledge.

Whitehead, S. and O'Connor, P. (2022) *Creating a Totally Inclusive University.* London: Routledge.

Whitehead, S. (2022) *Total inclusivity at Work.* London: Routledge.

On Self and Identity

Dent, M. and Whitehead, S. (2001) *Managing Professional Identity: Knowledge, Performativity and the 'New' Professional.* London: Routledge.

Whitehead, S. (2012) *My Dark Side.* Luton, UK: Andrews.

Whitehead, S., Talahite, A. and Moodley, R. (2014) *Gender and Identity: Key themes and new directions.* Oxford: Oxford University Press.

Whitehead, S. (2024a) https://medium.com/wokeup/two-billion-single-people-not-a-lot-of-sex-74f08424fc22. 10 September.

Whitehead, S. (2025) *Design Your Self, Love Your Self: 21 life lessons learned the hard way.* Cambridge: Pegasus.

Whitehead, S. (2025b) *The End of Sex: The Gender Revolution and its Consequences.* Luton, UK: Acorn Books.

On Relationships

Whitehead, S. (2003) *Men, Women, Love and Romance.* London: Fusion Press.

Whitehead, S. (2012) *The Relationship Manifesto.* Luton, UK: Andrews.

On Education

Whitehead, S. and Moodley, R. (1999) *Transforming Managers: Gendering Change in the Public Sector:* London: UCL Press

Machin, D. and Whitehead, S. (2020) *International Schooling: The Teacher's Guide.* Bangkok: Pedagogue.

For a full list of Stephen Whitehead's publications including academic and mainstream articles, plus podcasts and videos, go to:

www.stephen-whitehead.com

Additional Bibliography

Burn-Murdoch, J. (2024) https://www.ft.com/content/29fd9b5c-2f35-41bf-9d4c-994db4e12998. 26 January.

Dotinga, R. (2016) https://www.cbsnews.com/news/more-women-report-same-sex-relationships/. 8 January.

Hill Collins, P. and Bilge, S. (2020) *Intersectionality*. Cambridge: Polity.

Klein, J. (2021) https://www.bbc.com/worklife/article/20210610-why-more-women-identify-as-sexually-fluid-than-men. 15 June.

Also from Stephen Whitehead

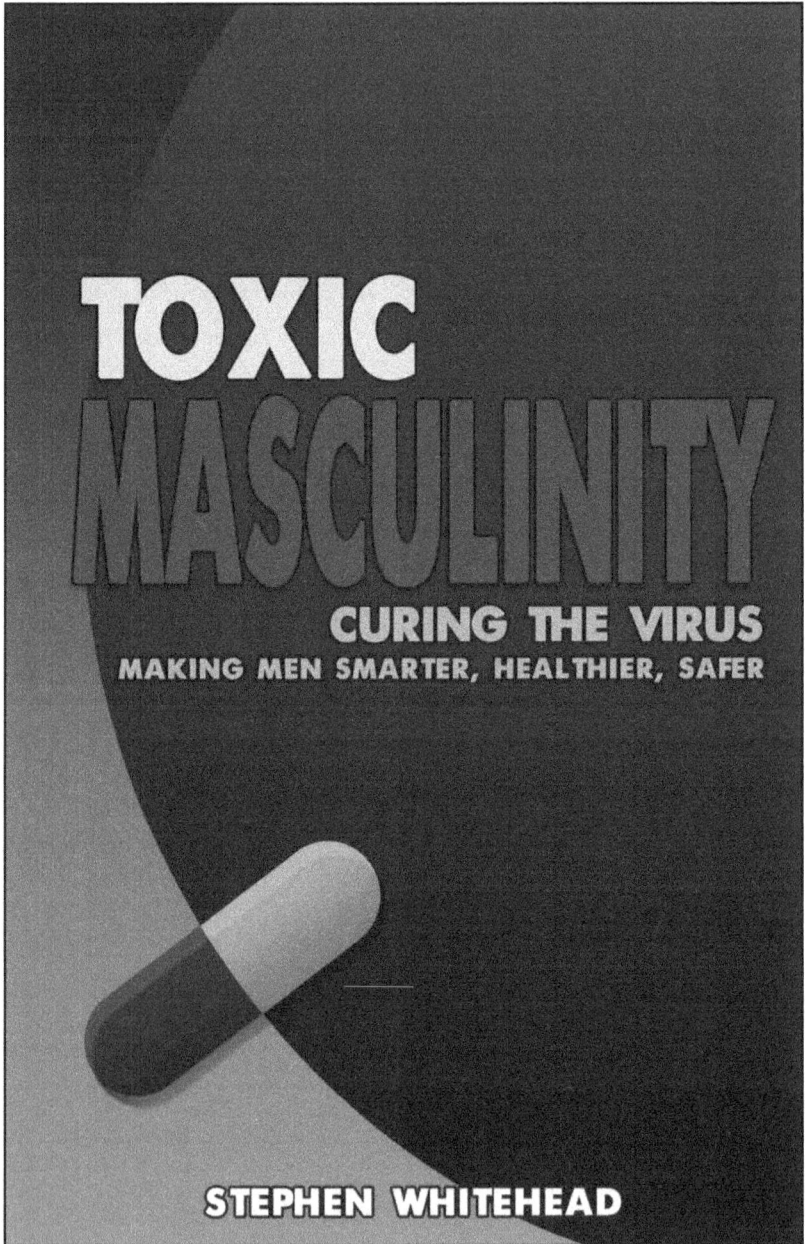

TOXIC MASCULINITY

CURING THE VIRUS

MAKING MEN SMARTER, HEALTHIER, SAFER

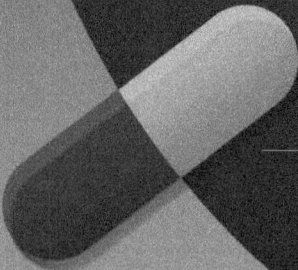

STEPHEN WHITEHEAD

www.ingramcontent.com/pod-product-compliance
Lightning Source LLC
Chambersburg PA
CBHW022356280326
41935CB00007B/209